FOREVER AGAIN

My Search for Unconditional Love

Benjamin Greggory

Copyright © 2015 Benjamin Greggory
All rights reserved.

ISBN13: 978-1508448600
ISBN10: 1508448604

CONTENTS

Introduction 1

Grains of Sand 4

Under the Influence 24

What You Ride?! 34

Hurry up this way again! 42

A Kiss Is Just A Kiss 50

Belladonna 61

Ask JS! 65

Shaken, not Stirred 77

Baby! Baby! Baby! 79

Hey DJ 95

Ready Or Not? 113

The Elle Train 123

Just like Candi 143

I Wish I May…, ... 159

One More Chance 175

Keep It On The Table 179

Anna One, Anna Two… 191

Seeds of Resentment 197

Three's a Crowd 207

And Then There Were NONE 213

Onward 215

One More For The Road 219

Introduction

It's 3am, I'm tipsy and I just pulled up in the front of my place. I'm jumping radio stations trying to find something relaxing, but smooth. My rearview mirror lights up. There's a car pulling up behind me. I roll down my window and hold out one finger as if to say, "Hold on!" I take a sip from my flask, not that I needed it, but I know it'll keep me where I wanna be. Another car pulls up on the other side of the street. I step out of the car, take one last long drag from my square, adjust my suit jacket, and then pop in a fresh stick of gum. Showtime! I bust a devilish grin, and casually stroll to the ride behind me (after all they were here first). I open the driver side door and double step over to let out the passenger. Then, I saunter across the street and open yet another driver-side door. Now I'm standing at my front door... *ME AND 3 VERY ATTRACTIVE LADIES..* All waiting. Waiting to be fulfilled, relaxed, and entertained. Let the games begin. It's 3:17 am. This *is* my life.

FOREVER AGAIN

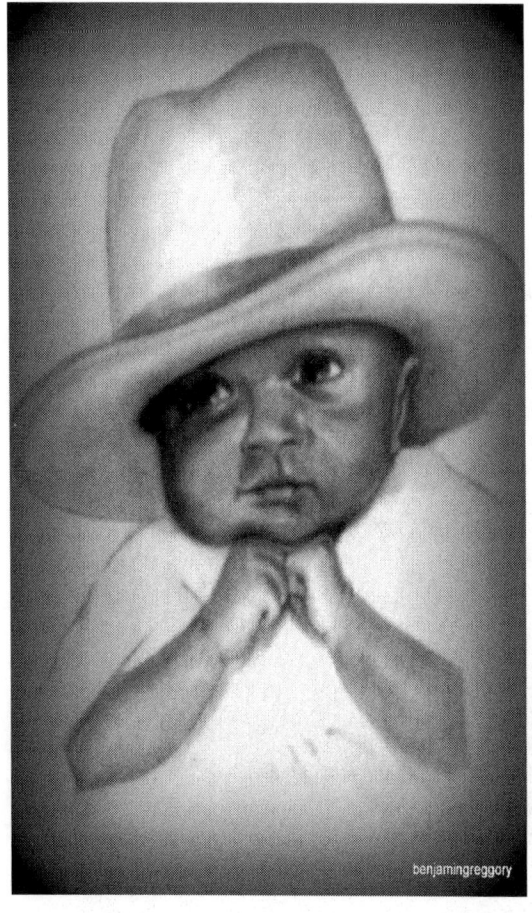

Grains of Sand

I considered myself a player, but not your *average* player. I was more like the Michael Jordan of players. And as the years progressed, due to both injuries and personal growth, I made adjustments. In doing that, I've had a legendary run… and even managed to win a few championships.

So you may be thinking, instead of comparing myself to #23, I should try maybe a Satchmo or Dizzy Gillespie – cause I like to toot my own horn – but I used MJ 'cause he once said, "People don't think about the shots I've missed, just the score at the end of the game." When I heard that I immediately thought about all the dates, girlfriends, fiancées, and yes, the one-night stands I've had over the years. And I stopped to ask myself, "Have I won any championships?" I mean, I could rationalize my claim by saying that bumping the baddest chick in the club, or sleeping with three women in one day, or even having two girlfriends at once - *NOT YOUR "AVERAGE" SITUATION, MIND YOU*. The kind where they don't know about each other, two girlfriends, I mean all three of us eating, sleeping, and playing together two girlfriends would be validation enough. My ego tells me that in 'playerdom' those are victories. But here's the rub, as much as I sometimes hate to admit it, I have a heart! I know right?! Go figure! It's the very antithesis of my ego and it tells me that all I've won were consolation prizes and parting gifts. I was that dude on Wheel of Fortune, who leaves with a version of the home game! I totally get it now though! , I think if we all conducted our relationships the way we drive newly acquired cars, we'd all be in mint condition emotionally. When you're driving and you see a red light you stop... but, when you get that same signal with your significant other. You run right through it! At times, I've even stopped cold! When I've clearly seen that the light is green. So, it's either start paying attention to these signals... or keep crashing into shit! I've always looked at the male female dynamic like two people running a race, imagine, the starting pistol goes off! They're neck and neck for the first lap... then fueled by her perception of a win, she begins to overtake the man by several laps. The question she has to ask herself when she looks back and doesn't see the emotional slow poke she started with, AM I WILLING TO WAIT or SHOULD I KEEP RUNNING to the finish line; and maybe try again WITH A GUY THAT"S MORE MY SPEED!. Ironically, the guy she started with is coming... just not at her pace. No, there certainly isn't a guarantee that he'll have enough emotional wind left in him to pick up the pace as she jets out of sight. However, my opinion is, if she wasn't willing to exhibit genuine patience (by that I mean not her perception of patience, but a fair presumption) why did she decide to run with him. If she's not careful, she'll cross the finish line 1st alright... and she'll be the last to find a mate as opposed to her girls who have learned to slow down.

Let's backtrack, shall we? See, I often compare myself to fictional characters, Neo in the Matrix Trilogy, for example – because although he *had* the innate ability to be "The One", initially, he didn't recognize it. And, because when others told him *they* believed he was "The One", he humbly refused to accept it. Now, before you think to yourself, "This is one egotistical MF!" hear me out.

All I mean is that, because a cloud of humility has always hung over any talent, ability, or positive attributes I've had, my existence has been mediocre – to say the least. But once *I* started to believe, I felt like nothing could stop me! I've never been one that was gifted with great opening lines – but I did have "Presence", or as they say now, "Swag." I was once told by a gorgeous woman, that "I usually date guys that are tall and muscular…," which made me feel some kind of way. But, she went on to say, "… your swag is like 6'7' and 280lbs!" Now I never stand in the mirror like, "HELL YEAH!" so that statement came to me as a shock; especially coming from someone who was arguably the finest woman there that night. But, I thought about it, and people have *always* said things like that to me. And admittedly, I knew that my "Presence" could incite love, hate, respect, admiration, and even intimidation of both men and women. –Women love me, men admire me.

Conventional game is written in stone, but one thing I've learned, pulling a woman is 10% what you say and 90% what you don't. Now, when you factor in a high swag, you create a tool that players worldwide hold in high regard – MYSTERY! Naturally, I walk kind of funny – as noted by my uncle who pulled me aside one day and said, "Y'know, if you wanna get a *real* job, you're gonna have to stop be-boppin' when you walk!" As a result, when I'm out, I literally watch my step! I know I can't spark a conversation (at least not a genuine one), with just anyone, so I use quips and interject clever statements, then quickly shut the F**K up!

There are two sides to every coin. In my case, the head's side is a nervous goofball who is ready to run home when I'm *forced* to socialize. But, on the tail's side, is a meticulously well- groomed gentleman who walks with purpose, and speaks when necessary. This is my life.

I often wonder how I got to this point. In Buddhism, it is believed that the mind is an empty glass, and each moment of your life is like one grain of sand that has fallen into that glass. If that *is* the case, I should probably hit Target to see if they've got a nice set of tumblers for sale.

As I recall, when I was around four years old, I lived in a small town called Anderson, Indiana with my mom and dad. I had a ball! I was a happy kid, smart as a f*ckin' whip – if I do say so myself. I didn't miss a trick. So, when my dad took me over to his mistress' house to do his *business*, I had no choice but to absorb my fathers' shenanigans. Once there, they disappeared into another room for an amount of time, which, even for a kid, seemed way too long. Being a ***mother's*** son, I reported this tryst to headquarters. Then, I immediately began to exact my revenge on the- old man through a series of well-planned, carefully executed "incidents" that would have made Damien proud. It would be my first meeting with chivalry. You know the kind – that old-school, "You have dishonored my mother, now you will answer to me!" chivalry. So, when we finally got home, it was payback time! You see, my dad *conveniently* needed to take a shower as soon as we came in – I wonder why. I quickly plotted my revenge, and put my plan in FULL effect. I took my toy plane and broke it into pieces. There were different safety regulations back then, so THIS toy plane was metal! I jammed the sharp scraps into the cracks of our wooden floor, then went to the bottom of the stairs and yelled for my daddy to come down. Well, when he came out of the bathroom – that, by the way, *was conveniently located at the top of the stairs* – to see why I was screaming, he stepped onto a floor riddled with my razor sharp vengeance. As he tumbled down the stairs, I remember thinking "THAT was for me, and my mom!" My point is, that the whole period of my life, residing in Indiana, put handfuls of sand in my glass – not the beautiful white sand found on tranquil, pristine island shores of the Caribbean, but the slimy, greasy, polluted sand found on the tainted shores of the Gulf Coast after the BP Oil Spill.

But let's move on. My parents separated. My mom – now pregnant with my baby sister – and I are headed to the south side of Chi-Town. I found myself in the middle of the hood, and this was *nothing* like Indy. It was like I was starring in a waaaay off Broadway production of Cooley High! "El" trains pimps, hoodlums, junkies and constant "noise" replaced the tranquility I had come to know in Anderson, and *nothing* was like it used to be. At my new school, I stood out like a sore thumb. I was smart, cute, and spoke *proper* English. Right away, I had friends and enemies. Most of the girls were my friends; and the boys, my enemies. *This* was my induction into the game of "'playerism'" and "hateration".

Now there was always a kid who wanted to kick my ass. After all, I had a lot of nerve standing around minding my business looking all cute and stuff. I was asking for it, right? Oddly, without any training or experience I won most of my fights, which made the "IT" girls take notice.

The prettiest girls were off limits at this point. It was as if they felt I hadn't yet proven myself worthy of them. Still, they kept me on standby. At age 10, as I approached the middle of fifth grade, my classmates and I prepared for the annual gym show. That's an assembly put on by the Physical Education teacher who had nothing better to do. Interestingly, I focused on gymnastics, which, in retrospect, was a peculiar choice since he hadn't really taught us any. Luckily for me, I'd spent countless hours honing my gymnastics skills on the pissy mattresses that my guys and I had pulled out of the dumpster and set up in the coal yard behind the projects where we lived. We would spend the whole day flipping', competing with each other even, with no regard for the stories those nasty ass mattresses had to tell. Needless to say, I was more than ready for the show. At the end of my performance, the gym teacher approached *me* and asked if I'd be interested in heading a gymnastics team for the school. He explained that *we* would perform at the basketball games. I humbly accepted his offer, picked a few of my buddies that could flip, and before I knew it, the "It" girls were mine *all* mine! I juggled five or six girls that "liked" me, while fielding a few "Would you go with me?" notes a week. Kim was the prettiest hands down, with her hazel eyes, Joi, was really cute, with her long curly hair and dimples, and Michelle; every school had a Michelle… that girl who *developed* early! I realized that in order to survive this onslaught of girls, without getting my eyes scratched out, I needed something. Finesse! Nobody pulled me aside to teach me about *finesse*, but among the older guys I'd watched and the pimps, players and "hoes" around the hood, once again, I observed and absorbed. I treated all of them well, with sensitivity and discretion – finesse. The only possible episode might have been the 5th grade school dance. So, I rolled solo. Somehow, I knew that my *best* move would be to work the room. I needed to keep them guessing, and keep my options open. Not bad for a fifth grader, huh? From that point on, *I* was a player.

Now, back to my Jordan reference – initially my game was pretty raw. I had a strong defense, but offense suffered because I was so eager to shoot I took a lot of unnecessary shots!. In other words, while I could get a girl's attention and bring out the "woman" in her, second base was totally not happening. I didn't even know there was a 2nd base. I was kinda stupid, luckily for me – and them. What I mean is that for a long time, I'd heard my friends chanting a ghetto rhyme which contained the phrase "she got bacon and eggs between her legs" subsequently I thought girls actually had bacon and eggs between their legs, why else would my friends be saying that, And what's not to like about breakfast foods right?!. So, most of my 'playerdom,' at that time, was innocent fun. A kid in the 70's – cute face with a big, dumb ass afro – how could I not have fun? I had two super cool best friends, a T.V in my room, a bike, and girlfriends. Those were good times. In reflection, Ever since my first kiss, I've had at least one, but more like two girlfriends. Maybe that's just how I'm made. When I was in the second grade, our teacher had to leave the classroom for one reason or another. As I recall, this little "It" girl decided she would mimic our teacher to pass the time. She started to ask questions about what we were learning. When she got to me, being the Aries that I am, I refused to answer because *she* wasn't our real teacher. Apparently, this was exactly the RIGHT response, because she decided to discipline me.

Off to the coatroom! I stood in the corner waiting'; maybe I wasn't that smart after all. When she came to admonish me for being "bad", she gave me a long deep kiss, tongue and all! I didn't blink. I followed her lead, and as you can see, I still remember it to this day. So, was I born some sort of oversexed "Freak" or does the "grains of sand" theory apply?

I was really having a great life in my new city. I left the catholic school (my mom who taught there part-time got a position at a public school) that's when shit got real! There were big kids here! I quickly discovered that the issues with socialization were the same, just different people. New school, new friends, new girls, and new mortal enemies – you know, typical kid shit. My next door neighbor was real cool. He had great toys and a classic ghetto mom who worked a lot and did her best for her kids. My neighbor's big brother was maybe seventeen; we were both eleven. One night, his brother had this girl over, a classic 70's beauty – I'm talking soul train dancer HOT. She was GORGEOUS! We spied on them. We watched them getting high, kissing and stuff in the front room. OOOOOOOOH! After a while, for some reason, my friend's brother left the house. But, his girl was still in the front room. All I remember is her saying was, "Y'all can get some too, and she was apparently being generous with all that she had to offer as a woman." (*YAAAY! Bacon and Eggs,*) So we did, there we were, like puppies rushing eagerly too feast on her ample tits.

This was the first time I had ever felt a woman up, so *that* was cool. I watched in awe as my buddy eased down to where she was sitting on the floor. And then, WHOA! He kissed her, like for real, for real, with tongue and everything! After some mild cajoling, she convinced *me* to come closer. I did, and she proceeded to lay a REAL wet one on me! WHAT A NIGHT! Now, Don was my best bud. We were thick as thieves. My mom even decided to let me sleep over at *his place* because he would invite me all the time. WE had big fun! We ate good food, stayed up late watching Creature Feature, and even dipped into his mom's stash of Vodka, which we not so cleverly replaced with water! Which led to the dreaded, ***even though I found out three days later I'm about to whoop y'all ass!*** asswhoopin!. But I digress!

Later on, in the wee hours of the morning, he decided that it was bedtime so like boys do we slept head to foot. But then, during my sleep, he began to touch me! I was too dumb to know what was happening at first. But the second time, not only did I realize I wasn't wit' it, I understood his predatory nature. We never spoke again. Every now and then, I think back on that time in my life, and wonder if or *how* it affected my growth as a person.

It's always interesting to speculate how I might've turned out had I been "unaltered". But, you've got to work with what you've got, I suppose. These types of events can be game changers, or are they signposts – marking your particular path. The projects were teaching me every day; these were life lessons that could only be learned the hard way! I had already been lured into sexual encounters, and little did I know that drugs and gangs were soon to follow! Needless to say, it's these kinds of events that add more of that slimy, gooey sand to my glass.

As a boy, my summer vacations were spent with Grammy, my grandmother, in Phoenix Arizona. These trips were a welcome escape from the south side. No pimps or junkies, no thieves or hoodlums, just me and my sister and the residents of her retirement complex. My Grammy had a caretaker who came by to attend to her needs from time to time. Since this guy seemed cool, Grammy gave the ok when he invited me to stay at his place. He had two girls and a big house. Grammy felt like I shouldn't be cooped up in an old folks' home all the time, so off I went. I always had a blast! This guy stayed on the go, so I got to see a lot of Phoenix. His wife was, in a word, awesome! She was kind, attentive and gorgeous! I definitely had a crush on her! His daughters were just as cute and funny as possible. In our travels, he took us – his daughters and me – to his buddy's house for a swim in the backyard pool. Seeing as how the average temperature in Phoenix reached 105 degrees, going for a swim worked for me. As it turns out, his buddy also had two girls; one of them, Kelly, just happened to be my age. Despite the things I had experienced, I was still a typical kid. But when Kelly came out to the pool in her two piece swimsuit, I felt something. I wasn't sure what *it* was, but I was sure *it* revolved around her bikini (which, as I recall, was a little small for her "budding" attributes). Kelly was a Hershey bar brown, with big dazzling eyes, and sumptuous lips. Our episode unfolded organically. A bunch of kids, playing in the pool – Splashin' around, doing cannonballs and stuff pretty typical summer fun. I hadn't paid attention, but the adults had gone inside, probably because it was so fuckin' hot! I guess that was Kelly's cue to show what she *really* was on! She bet me that she could hold her breath, under water, longer than I could. Being the competitive Aries boy— that I was (and still am), my response was basically… no freaking' way! So, we went under a couple times, smilin' at each other underwater, having fun. Then, and she started making' faces and even trying to tickle me into submission. But, her antics didn't work. I WON! So, she proposed a different challenge. "I bet I can dive better than you" she says to me. "Not possible", I responded, "but let me see what you've got!" As I mentioned earlier, I can be totally oblivious to flirting. In this case, I attribute it to the innocence of youth. But even now, I know I'm prone to watching a woman's advances fly straight over my head! When she suggested that I hold my breath while she dove in, it sounded awesome! I'd get to see her dive in… right? Wait a minute! How could I see her dive if *I* was underwater!? What a dumbass! What I did see though, was her thick frame, splash into the water. And, when the bubbles cleared.... TITTIES! Her bikini top had magically come off when she dove in! Something, I'm sure, she knew, would happen. As we surfaced, she said – clutching her chest, "Since you won the contest, would you go down and get my top?" Well, (cue hero music) "Okay!" I said. I got a big mouth full of air, shot to the bottom of the pool, and snatched her "lost" bikini top. Then, I sprang up from to the surface. After all, this was an emergency! As I handed her the bikini top, she smiled. That's when I realized how pretty she was. The sun bounced off the water on her chocolate brown skin, making her seem to glow. Now I know that the effect was actually due to the overabundance of chlorine that her father had put in the water! But, at the time, it seemed incredible! "Thank you", she said, "C'mon, I wanna give you your reward!" I said "Great, I'm starving, so YES! A sandwich would be on time!" We trudged our wet bodies into the house where she asked her dad if she could set up the Mouse Trap game in her room so we could all play. Dismissively, he told us to go ahead, but to be sure and clean up afterwards. I noticed that there had been no mention of sandwiches, but Mouse Trap was an awesome game, so "Whatever," I thought. See how dense I can be? When we entered her room, she closed the door behind us, then turned to me and said, "Did you like what you saw?!" "What?" I said. And as her smile washed away, a different look covered her face. "These," she said, as she pulled up her top. Her breasts popped out! Before I could say anything, she was right in front of me, on the floor. She grabbed my hand and placed it on her wet glistening chest, leading in the motion that she wanted me to go! As I continued, she began to kiss me, and I loved it! Now her hand was creeping' up the leg of my swim trunks, and she kept rubbing and stroking while we kissed. She stopped momentarily to reposition herself and stick one of her breasts in my eager mouth. As I suckled her, she stroked me until I exploded! Then, as she handed me her towel to wipe up with, she smiled and said, "You want something to eat?!" I laughed as I responded, "YES! I'm starving!" That summer, we did a lot of hanging' out at the pool, and it always led to something delightfully freaky. But, when the summer ended, so did our fling. There were many times, as a kid, when I went somewhere with an adult and encountered a girl with a freaky agenda. My entire formative years were peppered with steamy sex scenes, no drama just hotness.

FOREVER AGAIN

Maybe I was a born player.

Under the Influence

To be a *true* player, you must embody a plethora of attributes, which can only be achieved through the mentorship of an old-school player, and your innate ability to cultivate whatever gems were shared.

My dad wasn't around, in a very 'fatherly' way. There were no baseball games or bike rides, no skipping rocks on the water, or camping in the back yard. But, my dad *was* there for a lot of people. Ironically, he was the Big Boss – the HNIC if you will – of a non-for-profit organization whose focus was to empower inner-city youth. As I look back on our father-son relationship, I find his level of hypocrisy immeasurable. That notwithstanding, as a boy – like most boys do – I idolized my "old man". He was intelligent, charming, handsome, well-dressed and eloquent. Strangely enough, when I first saw our 42nd president strut to the microphone to speak for the first time, I was taken aback by the shades of similarity between them. And then, I was frightened by the thought that their swagger seemed so familiar.

Getting back to my point, my old man had a lot of the qualities I admired. And, while I *was* able to absorb bits and pieces of most of his more useful traits, that wasn't good enough for a young player. I had to refine them, and make them my own. Only then could I use *his* talents to achieve the next level of 'playerdom'.

As early as I can remember, I liked for my clothes to match. As a kid, I was *totally* on board the whole Garanimals thing. I would say I was *"clean"*, but being a boy, meant washing up as necessary! The important thing was looking good. Having my own style, involved everything from swiping my dad's blazers to cutting up my jeans and putting safety pins all over them. I wanted to be different. I wanted to have my dad's savior faire. I saw his pipe-smoking, black activism as super cool. And, when he went "corporate", the accoutrements – his brief case and company car – I considered a staple of success.

As a teenager, I used to attend a banquet with the old man, once a year. This annual celebration was held in honor of superstar pro football players. I really had a ball! I got to wear a tuxedo, and stay in a suite that was left over from the event planning week, at a prestigious hotel. Naturally, I took full advantage of the fact that because I was young, black, and donning a tuxedo, people – mostly white people – assumed that I was a football player. PERFECT!

One year, as I was getting on the elevator, and a voice called out "Hold the elevator!" I caught the door, and there stood a tall 'Sistah' with amaretto skin, a huge smile, and an Afro-centric wrap on her head. This lady was amazing to look at, and stood six-feet tall in her heels. She introduced herself as Risa, and struck up a flirty, Kind of dingy conversation on the ride up. She ended our conversation by telling me how she was so late, and how she didn't even have time to fix her makeup. Well, being the gentleman that I am, I offered to let her use *my* suite to refresh herself. Honestly, I didn't know what to do while I was waiting, so I just watched some television – the grown up kind. I didn't want her to think I was just some stupid kid who loved to watch cartoons all the time! 'What sophisticated gentleman does that right?

She called my name from the bathroom and said she needed a hand. When I got there, she greeted me with a big topless hug! She had an endearing; ditzy way about her that I figured was a clever way to disguise her obvious intelligence. That shit worked! She asked me if I would play with her before she went to the banquet, and with a mouth FULL of titty, I literally couldn't say no! Before I knew it, my pants were around my ankles and she was giving me some 'I've been training to get me a ballplayer' style head. I was on top of the world! She finished, tidied up, and we headed to the banquet. On the way, we got stopped by the photographer. Clearly, by walking with this woman, the masses figured I must be a ballplayer! We took a few pictures, she gave me her number and a kiss on the cheek, and that was that.

I couldn't wait to show the pictures to my old man, and tell him how much fun I was having. When I caught up with him, he rather matter-of- factly said, "That's not what I gave you the key to the room for." The next weekend, my dad came by the house to take my sister to an amusement park. When he came in, he told me that he had something in the car for me.

Now, my dad was NO slouch when it came to gifts so I knew it was something cool. I rushed outside to see what it was. As I got closer, I saw someone sitting in the passenger's seat. The smile seemed familiar. It was Risa, the chick from the banquet! Devastated, I said a dry, "Hey." Then, I went back inside. My dad said that it was best that I "stay a kid and let the men handle women". Right then, looking into my own father's eyes, something left me. I didn't know what it was, but I knew it was gone. Whatever *it* was, got replaced with a cold, callous viewpoint - THIS FOOL IS TRYIN' TO MAKE ME FEEL SMALL, WHILE HE'S PAYING FOR WHAT I GOT FOR FREE!". Unfortunately, the old man wasn't much more than a proverbial taxi driver; one who drops you off at the airport and doesn't care what plane you get on or your destination, because he's done with his responsibility. Despite this, and many other, instances of fucked-up-Ed-ness, the positive attributes my dad *did* have, surfaced in me. They would prove to be cornerstones of my "playerism".

The next strong male influence I recall is my uncle Lucky. In my eyes, this dude was the epitome of cool. He was suave, sophisticated, cultured – the whole nine. Lucky was who *I* wanted to be. He was always super clean, well-spoken, and cool - but not "Hood cool"- Nat King Cole cool. I wanted to have substance, like my Uncle Lucky, not just the ability to 'pull' women based on my looks. Since I've never felt I was 'cute', I figured I'd need all the help I could get. I was always listening or watching when my uncle was around. I still do! He would talk about politics, sports, the theatre, great desserts, and wines; and there I was, soaking it all in!

I remember once, my Mom, Sister I; went to a penthouse restaurant near Lucky's place. You can't imagine how cool I thought this was, especially coming from the Projects. We had to travel all the way to the North Side. For those of you not from Chicago, the North Side was 'where it's at'! We get to Lucky's place –an upscale bachelor pad. His place was so elegant you that immediately thought to yourself, "Do Not Touch ANYTHING". I was amazed at his expensive Asian influenced motif, and his awesome stereo. He even had – get this – a VCR with a wired remote control. How awesome is that! The trip to the restaurant *was* my inception to 'playerdom'. I belonged in this world, or so I thought. That impression irreversibly molded my thought patterns. Now, thirty something years later, whenever a woman comments on my grooming, attire, or ability to fit in (whether I'm on the block or at a high-class restaurant) I immediately think, "Thanks Lucky." How else would I have learned about suits, ties, cufflinks, colognes, shoes, overcoats and so on? It's funny, a woman recently told me, "I'm not used to talking to a man of your caliber." I thought, "What the f*ck is she talking about!? I'm just a work-a-day guy, with a meager existence – just sneaking by!" Then later, it hit me. I had become like my uncle. You see, with all of his style and elegance, the sharp clothes, cultured events, and suave sophistication, my uncle worked. I mean, he *really* worked. He was a train conductor for the Chicago Transit Authority for 30 years! That's when I realized, a *real* player defines his life, instead of letting his life define him, and I was forever liberated - *again*. Thanks Lucky!!!

Now, on to Mr. Drake, who was a friend of my Mom's; He was an older dude with an over the top persona that made him super cool. He was always talking about acting, art, or how to beautify something. This dude even wore an ascot, and drove a convertible Mercedes-Benz. Mr. Drake made me realize that this cool thing would have to last a *long* time. At this stage in the game, I'm a combination of my male influences, and the neighborhoods where I grew up. This doesn't make me feel 'cool', that would be arrogant. No, I feel DIFFERENT. Different in the sense that sometimes I don't know exactly where I belong! I'm not quite a thug. Nor am I bourgeois. However, I can survive – even thrive – in both worlds.

I recall going into a local bar one night. I was all 'thugged' out in my New York Yankees fitted cap, jeans, Nike Air Force One gym shoes, and black leather jacket; the whole rip. I sat there for like an hour surrounded by the same waitresses and patrons, as always. Only one of them recognized me! I ended up heading home (1 block away) and when I got there I decided to put on my "going out" clothes. I stopped back by the lounge and was greeted like Norm on Cheers! So, I've come to the conclusion that whatever sex appeal I have depends greatly on what I'm wearing! Women have always tried to convince me of how handsome I am. I never buy into that. But, thanks to my mentors, I *do* have a style.

I have to admit, I feel some kind of way when women are attracted to me by my clothes, but f*ck it! Attraction's got to start somewhere, right? I guess you've got to use what you can.

What You Ride?!

Despite all the positive influences in my life, I still had to deal with the everyday reality of growing up in the hood. The projects had pros and cons of course, for example, there was a hierarchy that you had no choice but to respect. The Grandmas' were at the top; EVERYBODY respected their words with no question. Second in command were the parents, although they weren't always around, when dinner time came, your ass better be at the table, and if you *had* done anything wrong or right, they surely would've heard about it from the elders as they walked home. 3rd in line would be the young adults; since they presided directly over us they had the most impact. We looked up to them and of course emulated all of their ways, from the way they walked to the slang they used, good and bad, they were our template. As me and my best buddies became teens, the playground memories of merry-go-rounds faded.

We were left with the usual state of awkwardness, you know the kind where you still wanna play but it's no longer cool, so you just kinda hang around! That's when the BS began. Once, while we were all sitting in front of one of the more danger/excitement filled buildings, a guy walked up and interrupted our session of the dozens with a question that (based on our collective reactions) we'd never heard. "What y'all ride? Well my response was "huh?" and everybody else followed suit. "Y'all folks? We all looked at each other with dumb looks on our faces, and the oldest one of us (Tony) stood up and declared " All The Time!" as he threw up a gang sign. This was all new to us, hell; they might as well just have started speaking French! As their conversation continued the strange guy kept asking Tony questions like, "do you know so and so, or spit some laws!" (We later found out he was talking about the laws of the gang). Well, it turns out ole Tony *didn't* know so and so, or one single law, and once his cover was blown the whole atmosphere changed, like when a summer storm comes outta nowhere! The strange guy had suddenly become visibly aggressive, which was obvious by the way he smacked Tony's hat off his damn head and made him take his chain off and give it him!. As the guy disappeared off into the distance, Tony lifted his head and asked "why y'all didn't help!?" silence fell over the crew, and then almost like it was rehearsed we all just started laughing! Pausing to say stuff like "we thought you had the situation under control folks!" or "we didn't know you were getting robbed, you acted like you knew him and that we were squares!" After he had suffered enough humiliation Tony went to the building close to his family's place to lick his wounds. The realization we all had was simple, we were either supposed to be in a gang or we were *highly* "recruitable!" As I pretended to watch T.V later I wished I could talk to my Dad about this, but I knew he wasn't that kinda guy. Yep, I was on my own, with my mom fighting to keep me on the straight and narrow path, I resisted at every turn, insisting that she transfer me from the four star catholic school she was paying for to a public high school which I thought would be a better fit. I slowly made the transformation from sweet kid to young thug in a matter of months, I came home one day without my Afro! How?! Because I got a perm that's how! In the streets it was referred to as getting' your butter whipped! It didn't go over very well with mom though; as a matter of fact, she was *so* mad she didn't say a word! I felt like I could deal with her silent rage, and I got in the bed, only to be awakened by the screams of dear ole' mom, as she sat on my chest with a pair of sewing scissors and cut freshly whipped butter, the fuck outta my head!. I straightened out, but it didn't last long, kinda like moms' patience. One night after hanging' out in the streets I crept into our apartment *way* past curfew! As I slowly closed the door, I felt like I could make it to my room *without* waking mom. I had underestimated the ole' girl again! Because when the last tumbler in the door lock clicked (giving me a sense of relief) I turned to sneak into my room under the cover of total darkness. Oddly, I began to see flashing lights! Not real ones, the kind you can only see when someone starts swinging a broom handle at you while its pitch black and it connects! Moms' was not having' it! And furthermore, I had just purchased a one way ticket to Dad's house! This was cool, because I knew I could get away with EVERYTHING. No more gym shoes for this guy! Why? Because cool guys didn't play games, *that's* why! Now I had become a gang member, school was more of a business opportunity than anything else. You see while looking for some tools one day I found the old man's weed stash! Perfect! Not only could I get baked for free, but I could unlock my entrepreneurial spirit, so now I'm the weed man at school. No more classes, in fact, the only thing I had in my bag was a.38 caliber pistol, (also the old mans') plenty of weed to sell, and some smokes, oh! I forgot to mention that since my Dad had a habit of taking a couple of pulls off of a smoke and then snuffing it out, that I had begun to smoke his cigarette ashtray leftovers, but since I was making' money, now I could afford to buy my own! By this time I was fully immersed in the street life. If I wasn't starting a fight, I was with my guys, breaking into somebody's car or a house, snatching a chain, even stealing cars, I was out of control! One day after work (I mean school) I had gotten sloppy drunk off of a half pint of gin, somehow I managed to get on the right series of buses to my Dads' neighborhood, when

I got off at my stop, I stumbled three blocks, from the bus stop to the front door. When I got in I dropped my bag, and I must've fallen down the basement stairs and passed out! When I came to I was in deep shit all my secrets had been revealed! My dad now knew that I was selling weed, that I was gangbanging and of course that I drank and smoked squares. I suppose even he was at his wits end because he drove me to my grandmother's house. My grandmother (Mama) was a pastor, so I guess my Dad sought her spiritual advice. I could hear them talking in the kitchen, I was still woozy but fully aware. As I listened, my Mamas' pit bull (Bullet) ran out of the kitchen to let's say introduce himself! So now I'm sitting on the plastic covered sofa, half drunk with the only thing between me and this charging pit bull being marble coffee table (which to his credit he leaped over effortlessly!) as I raised my arm (luckily I'd never taken my coat off) Bullet tried to latch on!, as I began to bang his head on the coffee table, pausing only to respond to my Mamas' voice from the kitchen" Benji what are you doin?!" "Playing with the dog" I replied as Bullet faded to unconsciousness,

I placed his body under the table. My Mama then came out of the kitchen with a grape soda, and a ginger ale for me, Well, grape soda was my favorite, cool, and everybody knows ginger ale will to settle any stomach, got it. Mama began reading me scriptures from the Bible, and as she did I felt the room begin to spin. She kept reading the good book as she sat next to me, but as the room started to fade, I remember throwing up all over her, and what's more important, her bible!. I still bookmark that incident, and my grandmother really never spoke to me again! Until she was on her death bed; It was official I was a heathen! One who had just purchased a ticket back to his moms' house.

Hurry up this way again!

Now that I've gotten the preliminaries out of the way, let me tell you about the path I walked in the late 80's. I was still living at home and did a lot of hanging out. My mom bought a 2-flat, greystone apartment building – no small feat for a single, black mother of two. We weren't far from the projects where I'd grown up. But we were far enough! After the residing tenants – an elderly couple – died, she rented the upstairs apartment to her second set of tenants. They were a good "Christian" family of five: a husband, wife, and three daughters. They seemed nice enough, and everything was cool. Part of my summer routine was sitting on our front porch. I didn't have much else to do. Each day, the wife of the family would come home from work and give me a cheerful greeting. It was a confidence builder. I admit, she was sexy, and, I did have a slight crush. But, it didn't help matters when she'd stop and smile, and say – in her baby voice –"That baby sure is handsome; Hello my baby!" As you can imagine, I was hooked! Who doesn't like baby talk?

As the man of the house, I was in charge of making sure the tenants' needs were met. My responsibilities included opening the basement door, so the tenants could do their laundry. It was the laundry room where shit got real. At first, we would exchange pleasantries, and that progressed into casual discussion. Eventually, with the precision of a neurosurgeon, she began to lace our conversations with sexual innuendo. She slowly picked apart any game I *thought* I had. As we chatted, I would often *try* to flick my cigarette into a bucket about 10 feet away from where I stood. Sometimes I made it, sometimes not. One day she noticed and said, "If you get it in the bucket, I'll give you a kiss." So, I took my last puff, measured my shot, and flicked. Off it went, soaring straight into the bucket. I didn't really know how to react. I just looked at her and smiled. She walked over to me, grabbed my chin, looked into my eyes, and then deeply kissed my soul! As we kissed, her hands began to explore my young frame, gradually making their way to the center of activity. She caressed me gently, unlike anyone ever had before. Her touch was incredible. I felt intoxicated. I was flustered – filled with a nervous excitement! I was torn, but in a trance. The sound of my pants unzipping snapped me out of my drunken stupor. She carefully guided me out of my restraints, looked down, and with my whole self in her hands, she masterfully stroked me as she looked into my eyes. She smiled and said, "Ooh, you ain't a baby!" Now, I ain't gonna lie, my ego was quickly approaching Saturn, but moving too fast to take pictures. Then she kissed me softly, leaned to my ear and asked, "Can I kiss it?!" Well the best I could do is say, "Mmmm-hmm." She led me into the bathroom, with mys*elf* still in hand. As she skillfully unbuckled my pants they fell to the floor, she never got up. She forced me to sit down by digging her fingernails into my chest. She engulfed me, performing an oral feat that surely set the bar for all future competitors. As she took my length down her throat, she pulled my full young sack towards her wanting mouth gently, then she stuck her tongue out and tickled my jewels. She gagged, but only slightly. Then she rose, and softly said, "Nobody gives head like me!" Well, she would certainly get no argument from me! She descended to resume her phenomenal tongue ballet, and insisted that I give her my juice. I began to explode, and she reached up to put her hand over my mouth, fearing that my moans would give us away. I squirmed as she inhaled every drop. Finally, I was still, and she removed her hand. This was my introduction to the world of older women. We had many clandestine meetings. After that, I would intentionally wait for her to get home from work. When she'd finally arrive, we playfully assumed our roles, pretending we were *just* the landlord's son and the upstairs tenant. But all the while, I was learning how to slowly make love and enjoy a woman from head to toe. This was the woman who truly awakened what I call, my Level-4 foot fetish. Because of her, I love pretty feet. How they look in heels, and how they feel in my chest are crucial. And, yes, *suckable* toes are a must! Like Eddie Murphy's character in the movie Boomerang, whenever I meet an attractive woman, I always hope she has pretty feet! Jacked up feet is a deal breaker!

Still, there were more substantive lessons that I learned from my favorite upstairs tenant. She taught me that 'love' is totally subjective. You can rationalize yourself into some bullshit at any given moment. And, when you do, it certainly isn't real love. Although I appreciated *all* I'd learned during our tête-à-têtes, I knew they could not continue. I'd be leaving for college soon; I did manage to quell my hood shit thanks to two of my running buddies B- dog and Mace. One day a B-dog came to me and said that while he was visiting his girlfriend, in Chicago's infamous Stateway Gardens housing projects; he was smacked around by some opposing gang members. His eyes were red with revenge (um and he was drunk and high) he had a revolver and one bullet, and was on his way to pick-up Mace; they were headed back to Stateway. Knowing that this was a terrible idea, in my infinite stupidity, I insisted on driving. I figured that it would give time to talk them out of it! So much for that! We pulled up outside Stateway about a half a block from his girlfriends' building. They got out and ran into the building, I heard that one bullet he had, fire. The sound echoed through the projects. I was somewhat relieved to see them both running my way, time to get the fuck outta dodge! It was quiet as I drove what legally would be the getaway car, I dropped myself off and they peeled off. B-dogs mom, called later, I had been calling his house, and she asked me if I knew what happened, so I played dumb. She went on to say that as the guys pulled up at his house, police swarmed and arrested the both of them. When she asked what was going on, the detective said that his girlfriend (who was sitting in the backseat of the officers' car) had positively identified them as the perpetrators of a murder that had taken place earlier that day. As I hung up the phone, I went numb, I should've done more, I thought to myself. About a month later I received a letter from my dude, saying that this life wasn't for me, and to go back to school. He went on to say that he appreciated what I had done, and that his advice was his return of that favor. I knew that if he had said Gramps (my street name) was driving the car, I was a goner! But as a friend he wanted to let me know that there was more to life... my life was saved that day. I enrolled in an alternative high school, got my diploma and found myself in college 6 months later... fresh off the streets.

I wasn't in the dorm very long before I got a call from my mom. Her voice trembled, and she was clearly in shaken. She called to announce that the man upstairs had been missing for about a week and that she'd found him in our garage – slumped over in his car! He had stuffed a cloth in the tailpipe, started the engine, and waited. His body was swollen from Chicago's summer heat – and the time that had passed since his demise.

What had I done!? Had I inadvertently been complicit in giving my mother an indelibly haunting image? Had *I* destroyed a wholesome family unit? Had he found out about the affair? Had *that* prompted him to commit suicide? These are questions that I'll have answered. I will never know what *really* happened, or why he chose to end his life. Out of shame, I didn't attend the funeral. She and I never spoke again. And, although my tryst with his wife had long since ended, the weight of his death is something I still carry.

FOREVER AGAIN

A Kiss Is Just A Kiss

I was back from Southern Illinois University after 3 ½ years; and attending Columbia College here in Chicago, and working part-time at a hole in the wall electronics store downtown. As I recall, it was a slow day. I have been just chilling, and then *IT* happened. That's right, one of life's slow-mo-tion moments! SHE walked up and asked if I would show her a CD Walkman. *Remember those?* I was mesmerized by her skin, her exotic eyes, and her luscious LIPS. WOW! Her lips were unbelievable! It always looked like she was kissing. This woman had a great smile, and her body was reminiscent of an ancient Greek statue. My mom had always said, "Light-skinned girls are CRAZY!" But, I had to disregard that warning. Besides, how crazy could she be?

A couple of things were obvious right away. First, the guys tried to talk to her, ALL OF THE TIME – A LOT of guys. So, she was no stranger to bullshit. Second, my time was limited. Still, my approach had to appear organic. I had to speed up the natural progression of our conversation with a sprinkle of well-placed jokes, a dash of artful eye contact, and a dusting of the subtle flirtation. For example, saying "Let me help you with your headphones," then casually touching her hand while stealing a glance into her eyes, and showing her how to operate the piece of crap I was about to sell her!

About an hour later, I had gotten past the hurdles. I'd gotten a phone number, *and* had a date set up. Oh, and by the way, she didn't buy the Walkman, which really pissed off my boss! She was really just browsing anyway. I had convinced her to take a closer look at a Walkman while I felt her out. Advantage me! Just like most young guys, I was living at home and I didn't have a car. So, the most of my involvement with Asha was via telephone. But we had hours of great conversation. And, since her mom lets her use the car occasionally, she'd drop by.

After all, I had absorbed up to this point, there was still a hell of a lot for me to learn. You see, Asha had me OPEN. I mean, how rude she was! Imagine taking a young man in his sexual prime and dangling the cootie over his proverbial head for a few years! That's just MEAN!! My mentors hadn't schooled me on this one, and I had no one to call. I was on my own! What I didn't know, however, was that she was helping me define 'love'. See, I'd started to tell myself that the conditions weren't important, *only* the level of dedication.

As my 'relationship' with Asha progressed, I saw the feathers gently fall from my beautiful angel. I remember quite vividly inviting Asha to go skiing with me in Lake Geneva. When we arrived, the group leader called a meeting in the big Chalet the group had rented, you know, just to review some general information. They had prepared a nice spread of food and libation for us to enjoy. So, we sat and listened. When the presentation was over, we went back to our room where Asha says, "I have a surprise for you!" Given that, despite many valiant efforts to get to 'home base', I had yet to hit one over the fence, I convinced myself that her little 'surprise' was some skimpy lingerie or something ridiculously sexy. What she revealed was both disappointing and sobering at the same time, like being drunk at a fabulous party only to have someone call you to say that your dog had been hit by a car! Asha reached into her pockets and pulled out several packets of cheese, followed by four or five little bottles of wine. Nice! She had "stolen" shit that I had already paid for! If my beautiful master thief would have bothered to ask, our host would've happily fulfilled her desire for the cheap wine and cheese.

It was as if a big cloud blackened out the sun on a perfect summer day. And, it kept getting better – and by better I mean worse. While I was putting on my gear in the lodge, she leaned over and whispered "Look at these gloves I found." Looking at her in total shock, as kindly as possible, I pointed out that someone had merely put their gloves down and walked away for a just a moment – perhaps to get a lift ticket, or a hot chocolate, or I don't know what. Then I said to her, "PLEASE JUST PUT 'EM BACK WHERE YOU FOUND 'EM BEFORE THE AUTHORITIES GET INVOLVED!" Thankfully, she did, and we went off to ski. Despite all of her antics, we did actually have a relative amount of fun on the slopes. After a few hours, she was ready to head back to the lodge.

Since I love skiing, I didn't mind much, and stayed on the slopes. When I entered the lodge, it was like a camera ZOOMED in on me. Asha sat oblivious, surrounded by onlookers – softly whispering, chuckling, dumbfounded just watching. Her bare feet were propped up by the fireplace, and her socks were 'roasting' – like chestnuts – over the fireplace grate. SHEESH! My fallen star had given me nothing on this trip, except a lot of embarrassment. There was a moment, however. Back in our room, Asha decided to take a shower. Honestly, at this point, I thought 'WHATEVER'! But, when she came out in her towel, I couldn't help but peek. She had an athletic body – but not over the top – and she stood by the bed and called my name, playfully. "Ben-jer-minnnn!" I turned to look. She suggestively opened one side of her towel and walked slowly towards me, in her best burlesque style, flashing me with her Sally Rand show. When she finally got close enough that I could smell the Victoria secret body wash, she had bathed in, and she dropped her towel. I was awestruck! Her statuesque body was inspired by Venus. She casually reached over to the dresser and grabbed a bottle of baby oil. She handed it to me, and posed. With those luscious, pouty lips, she said, "I can't put this on by myself." I was eager to assist, and I slowly rubbed the oil over my goddess, careful not to miss a spot. I was given license to explore new territories, and as the massage continued, I found myself sucking her toes one-by-one. I caressed the space between her calves and thighs with my tongue, and playfully I nibbled her soft, succulent lips. "WAIT," she whispered, as I gently stroked the petals of her flower. "Ok baby," I replied, and we continued to passionately traverse each other with fingertips and lips into the wee hours of the night. Then, we wrapped our bodies together and fell asleep. That's right. With me being a 'believer' in *true* love, and waiting until we were both 'ready,' I settled for the occasional sessions of heavy petting which became typical encounter. This went on for years with Asha. And, for that time, she was my "true love." That being the case, I was fully prepared to spend the rest of my life with her. Unfortunately, the feeling wasn't mutual. See for me, I was in it for the long haul. She had me hook, line, and sinker. And then, the phone call – *cue ominous music*. Asha called one day and I felt a feigned sense of sorrow and trepidation in her voice. For some reason, I'm very in tune with the people's souls. After all, I had never been wrong about the "vibes" I got, from Asha. My spider-sense told me I was about to hear some, PURE–D BULLSHIT, as we used to say. So, I listened. And soon it was revealed that the love of my life had HERPES. At least, that's what she told me! HERPEEEZ! My first reaction, of course, was "PHEW! I'm glad you didn't give me any of that stale fish." But then, my dumb unselfishness kicked in. My response to the news went something like this… 'Baby, I love you, and no matter what, we can make it. Thank you for telling me the truth.' Now, here's why I said that. Part of me – my heart – believed what she said, and my heart had never failed me, when it came to uncovering the truth. That said, I knew that my response would either solidify our love, in her mind, or force her to be real with me. Well… she cried, and told me how thankful she was to have me. Blah, Blah, Blah, and things went back to normal.

Before she went back to school from summer break, I called her and asked to come over. When she got to my place, I had fake prepared a candlelight dinner. 'Fake,' because I had actually ordered it from an Italian restaurant giving the illusion that I'd cooked it myself – no different than when women pay for weave, and when YOU expose them, they say something like "It's mine, I got the receipt." Same shit! Anyhow, we ate, drank wine and enjoyed each other, as we always did. I gave her this ring I'd bought and asked her to marry me. SHE SAID YES! I was so excited! I was ready to JUMP THE BROOM; TIE THE KNOT; RIP THE RUNWAY; BREAK A LEG! You get the idea. We immediately got into another of our famous petting sessions, and life was good! A few months, an extraordinary amount of phone calls, and a few letters back and forth later, I received something that I thought was reserved for guys in the military – the infamous "Dear John" letter, written with the agility and balance of an Olympic gymnast.

Here's the gist of it:

"I'm not worthy of your love, and that's why I'm returning your ring...." She ended with the classic dismount, "I'll *always* love you." Her scores: 9.2, 9.0, and, a 9.5 from the Germans. As I suspected, she never had herpes. Her BFF later exposed that little tidbit. Asha just wasn't IN LOVE with me! Me!? There was no resistance from me though. At that point, I figured, I had embraced her fully and honorably. I remained by her side – Hee-bee-jee-bees and all, and to be lied to; was simply not acceptable. It was deeply hurtful, and made me feel that she was right, she was NOT worthy of my love. That was the last communication we had. And while, admittedly, my relationship with Asha did change my thinking; I did not change the way that I would love.

> Gregg,
> I am returning this because I don't believe I am worth having a piece of your soul. I ♥ U, I MISS U & I hope that we will soon talk & work things out. I know what it feels like to be hurt & disappointed, but our love for each can over-come anything --- that's if it's true love.
>
> Call when you're ready to talk
>
> "The blessing of the Lord be upon you."
> PSALM 129:8 NIV

BENJAMIN GREGGORY Bbenjamingreggory

Belladonna

I met Lana quite a while ago. She had a crush on me. In my infinite state of unawareness as to that type of thing, I thought she would make a good friend. She offered me rides to work, brought me lunch, things like that. She was real cool, y'know? As unscrupulous as I can be, I do TRY and respect the sanctity of friendship! So, out of respect, I never made any serious advances toward her. We did flirt, however. But, who doesn't… right? One night, she called and asked what I was up to. She asked if I would like some company for a while. "Sure," I said. After all, it's always cool to kick it with a buddy! "C'mon through," I told her. I made a quick run to the liquor store and grabbed a bottle of wine, then prepared for some good conversation. About 20 minutes later, Lana pulled up in front of my crib. I poured two glasses of wine and went downstairs to let her in. When she got out of the car, my whole damn tongue rolled out of my mouth – Wolfy style – straight out of a Tom and Jerry cartoon; a reaction I may not have noticed, except for the fact that my eyeballs had popped all the way out! It was a Lana like I had never seen, or even imagined! She looked good, damn good! She had on a sexily unbuttoned white cotton blouse tied in a knot beneath her glistening bosoms, a red mini-skirt that made my blood race, and black, open-toed, platform pumps completed her ensemble, if you don't include the scented oil that covered her body. As she approached, she saw a smile that stretched from the Atlantic Ocean to the Pacific. She opened her mouth and said, "I'm done playing' wi'choo!". I'm gonna wipe that smile off yo' face. Then you can finish your wine!" She pushed me into the vestibule and began to kiss me softly, but forcefully... passionately. She grabbed my face to stop me from reciprocating, then looked into my eyes and said, "You just let *me* do this!" I didn't respond; I just surrendered. She forced her hand down my pants and began to massage my jewels, running her fingers up and down the center of excitement. Soon, I realized I was no longer in the vestibule. I was LOST in another dimension! Lana pushed me onto the stairs and damn near yanked my pants off! She grabbed my man strongly at the base, looked at me with those beautiful hazel eyes, and licked my whole self. She feasted on my excitement until I was ready to explode. Then, she stood up, untied the knot in her blouse, and said, "I told you I wasn't playin' wi'choo!" She mounted my pleasure and slid down slowly, moaning softly. As her dance became more intense, she put her hand over my face, mashing my head into the stairs. I just closed my eyes and FELT. I caressed, and squeezed, and bit, all while anticipating her next touch. I smacked her on the ass – my attempt to signal her that I was ready. But, like a true first responder, she jumped off my pleasure, got back on her knees, and took the full force of my explosion! She stepped over me to climb the stairs, handed me my wine glass, and smiled. Lana looked at me and she softly said, "You shouldn't play so much." She and I are still friends to this day. We rely on each other in hard times. But, out of respect for each other, we don't have any episodes' these days. I do however; consider Lana… *a close and special friend!*

Ask JS!

My best friend was like my brother, to the extent we became roommates. He was an up-and-coming D.J., and we were always at a party. I gladly accepted the role of 'the other guy.' This particular night, he played a party at one of the local colleges. The crowd was "light", in terms of attendance, but the music was jamming'. Since I danced all the time, I hit the dance floor right away. Once upon a time, I had my own break dance crew – a story for another time. I was cool, just getting into a zone. That's when my dude put on "The Pee Wee Herman". I decided to show the sparse crowd how it's done!

Since women love great dancers, I quickly got their attention. The most engaging, Jasmine got mine. We talked for hours. She was heavy set, but *really* sexy (which is my only prerequisite). I thought she was Puerto Rican. She looked like the lead singer from Lisa and Cult Jam! I found out later that she was mixed. Her mom was ½ black and ½ Greek. Interestingly, she was the daughter of one of the most prolific black leaders of our time, a fact that gave me some insight as to who she was, and what she'd experienced. We shared the same sense of humor, interests, and ideals. She would drive her YUGO all the way from the North Side just to see me. And, in turn, I would take the long journey on the Green Line train ride to share her world. The first time she came by my place, it was early spring. It was nice out – a beautiful day. She had on this wrap around skirt and some mules, she smelled like fresh strawberries. As we talked, I couldn't keep my eyes off of her legs! I don't know if it was the way the baby oil made them shine, or the way she masterfully let her shoe dangle from her foot. Regardless, at that point, I knew that my status had been elevated to a Level 5 foot fetish! I gazed at her high arches. We drew closer as we talked, and I knew I had to touch her. So, I cracked a silly joke and, while she laughed, I ran my hand across her thigh, continued down to her calf, looked into her eyes and proceeded to remove her shoe. She had delicious, plump little toes that I could not wait to kiss. I could tell she was all in, so I put her barefoot foot in my lap where she would FEEL the intensity of my interest. That's when it hit me, I was attracted to the *SEXY*. There is no particular weight, height, skin-tone, or body type that moves me, but she (whoever she is) has got to have the *SEXY*! Before we knew it, we were in love. She asked me to move in with her. Since I was still living on my mom's back porch, I packed up my stuff and hit it! So there I was, 19 years old with a *real* girlfriend, full use of a car, and a *real* apartment – COOL! Jasmine loved me endlessly. I quickly got a job at a Sporting Goods Store downtown and began kicking in financially. We were perfect.

Let's talk for better or worse for a minute. My job required me to wear a uniform shirt. One day, foolishly, I had forgotten mine. So, I decided to borrow one that was in the locker room. BAD IDEA! The next thing I knew, I was all itching and scratching. I had LICE!

Jasmine was on it! She rushed to my job with a DE-LICE-IFICATION Kit already in the backseat of the car. When we got home, she painstakingly applied the ointment and with a magnifying glass, tweezers and a lot of love she picked lice off some very private areas until they were all gone. AMAZING! Looking back, I realize the ignorance of my youth. As a young man, I lacked reverence, and didn't *truly* understand how much love Jasmine had shown me.

Later in life, it turns out, I would desperately want (and need) this degree of loyalty; a woman who is nurturing, non-judgmental, and supportive. Jasmine was unconditional love, personified. My "game" would never be the same. Soon after, I changed jobs and became a telemarketer - the gig was closer to home. Everything was fine on the home front. I was very good at my job and, by and large, a very low profile guy. A friend at the time came to me with a plan to make some easy money. Apparently, he had a girlfriend that was dating a mid-level dope man. As he told it, while this guy was sleeping, she was swiping handfuls of his product and giving it to him. So, since we had this "stuff" with zero investment, we packaged it and became entrepreneurs. I had no idea that I would become so popular at work. The place was flooded with coke-heads! Classically, the girls who previously wouldn't give me the time of day were suddenly requesting "personal" moments with me. Of course I was overwhelmed by temptation and stupidity. I started having "parties" at our house while my girlfriend was working. Jasmine knew what I was doing. What she didn't know was that I didn't know what *I* was doing!

Enter Sinn – literally. She was older, by 10 years, with caramel skin, killer smile and ginormous breasts! One day at lunch, I was holding court in the cafeteria – cuz' by now, I'm the man. I noticed Sinn watching me. Although I'd been crowned "The Man", I was a kid. I was still a marionette, a puppet, a DUMMY, and raging hormones and lack of will were the strings. So, when Sinn pulled a cucumber out of her lunch bag and began to seductively devour it, I got all caught up! It was so enticing. She was so discreet. When she was sure no one else was looking, she would lick it, or kissed it, or something remarkably sexy! – I WAS GONE!! A brief conversation flushed out some important, need-to-know, details. She said she was married, and had a six year old daughter. I told her that I lived with my girlfriend. With those *minor* details out in the open, like most people on the brink an affair, we said to ourselves, "Fuck all that," and decided that we had to get together outside of work. Clearly, two assholes! But where would we meet? Sinn knew an idea! A mutual friend's house stays about a block from our office. It was a studio apartment, not much bigger than a closet, but it would have to suffice. We met there. We chatted for a while, and then she asked me, "What is your favorite part of my body?" One thing I had learned, as a player, was to never state the obvious. So, pointing out those enormous melons was out of the question! I simply replied, slowly, "I can't stop looking at those big... brown... beautiful – *wait for it*... eyes of yours." She laughed, and thought I was sweet. "Are you sure you haven't noticed these?" she asked, as she unbuttoned her blouse and removed her bra. Her ample 44 DOUBLE-DEEZ bounced down and back up, then just sat there! She wrapped the girls around my head and whispered, "You like 'em baby!" Of course, I could not answer with my face hidden in her chest – which, as you may have noticed, is a recurring theme for me. Still, it begs the question: Why do women always, wait until the *most* inopportune moment to ask a question - one that is, more often than not, rhetorical? Take your standard "Can I kiss it," for example. If you have my 'self' in your hands, why ask me? The answer will, undoubtedly, be YES! But I digress. Sinn grabbed a pillow from the bed and placed it on the floor in front of me. She knelt down and reached for my belt, as I leaned back in the chair offering NO resistance. She purred, "MMMMM," and that was the last time I saw my dick for a record breaking hour and a half. When she was done, she stood up and smiled and said, "Mmhmm, we're gonna' have fun together. Now c'mon we gotta go!"Go where?! I thought to myself... to get me a juice and a sugar cookie! Or maybe stop by the hospital and hook me up to an I.V?! Because CLEARLY I lost a lot of fluids! It was as if that whole session was merely a test of my stamina. I was glad I passed, but now I was a *cheater*. Sinn and I had dozens of after work rendezvous, and they were loads of fun. From her voyeuristic fellatio on the train platforms, to making love in the park, we did it anywhere and *everywhere*! It seemed that I now had a new and improved girlfriend. See, I started to lose my affinity for Jasmine, but I loved her. She had done nothing but love me, and she deserved whatever loyalty that I had left – and more. So, I stayed beside her. It wasn't like Sinn was going to leave her husband or anything, so this is just a fling, right? It happens all the time.

After a couple of years of creeping with Sinn, I got sloppy. I thought I was in love with Sinn – who by then had declared herself my *girlfriend*. She was saying things like, "I love you."…"I miss you."…"Why didn't you call me?"…"She got you so you can't call me!" Classic, I know, but I was knee deep in it now. My life at home, with Jasmine, was the same. It was disrupted, however, when I came up with the brilliant idea of sending Sinn some flowers. I bought them with the joint credit card belonging to Jasmine and me. Needless to say, when the bill came, I was busted. Jasmine tried to kill me – *for real*. When she tried to STAB ME, I grabbed the knife and ended up cutting three fingers – a fair alternative to what she was intending, I suppose. She started was screaming bloody murder, and called the police. I walked around the corner to call Sinn so she could come get me cuz' the cat was outta the bag. While I was on the phone, the police walked over. I lowered my voice and continued my conversation for about five more minutes. Surely the two police officers standing behind me was sheer coincidence... RIGHT? To my surprise, when I got off the phone one of the officers asked me if *I* was Ben. I said yes, and he politely handcuffed me and drove my dumbass back around the corner to my place to be identified – *by Jasmine*. At the police station, after a while of being locked up, the officer came to open the holding cell. I had been bailed out! He looked at me and made a comment that I will never forget. "Buddy," he said, "You've got one who put you in jail, and one who got you out. I know which one I'd choose". Then he gave me a pat on the back and wished me good luck! And I did choose – Sinn. It was as easy call, because Jasmine immediately portrayed the role of the embittered girlfriend. She immersed herself in it, and it was a stellar performance. She almost had me believing it – *almost*. Nevertheless, it was back to the South Side for me.

Now that I had left Jasmine, my oversexed – MARRIED - "girlfriend" wanted me all to herself! Sinn seriously didn't want me to see any other women! I was always quick to point out that she was married, which was completely beside the point. We had fight after fight, until I almost had to call the police and have her escorted away, for showing up at my place without permission and refusing to leave!

It came to me, finally, that I had been seduced… seduced by money, popularity, greed and lust. I had forsaken my love *and life as I knew it*, only to be left with a really expensive Life Lesson. **Respect yourself! If respect and fairness emanate from your core, negative decisions will be few and far between**. If you fall prey to temptation, you lose your integrity – your self-respect; and a man without integrity is nothing more than a grown child.

FOREVER AGAIN

Shaken, not Stirred

At this point, I'm 22 or 23 years old and back at the crib. However, there were a few modifications to my prior living arrangements. The tenants in Moms' building had moved out; so I moved into the second floor apartment. I didn't have any real "stuff" mind you. The television I purchased, while living with Jasmine, mysteriously disappeared when I asked if I could pick it up. So there I was upstairs, with home-made or second hand furniture, a pocket full of lint, and a head full of dreams. Strangely enough, I always had a girlfriend, or at least a steady F.W.B. (Friend with Benefits). Even though I had endured three losses, I chose to learn from the Jasmine situation, not to be bitter because of Asha, or be overly suspicious because of Sinn. At this point, I had a glass of sand with a little water in it. And now, I was more conscious of the fragility – and the strength – of love. I must admit, sometimes I wish I were one of those people who remained oblivious to bone crushing failure. But for some reason, I always reflect on these episodes, sift through the wreckage, mourn the passing, and cherish the core value of life's lessons – a trait that I've long perceived as both a blessing and a curse. People often say to me, "You're always so calm and cool." I just say "Thanks," knowing that the reason for my collected demeanor is that I've had my heart smashed into a billion pieces *and* had to sit for countless hours patiently gluing it back together, because I believe for some reason, that I may need all of the pieces. Yes, a *whole* heart is what I want to give. Still, I wrestle with how wrong or right, I may be.

Baby! Baby! Baby!

While I walked around in a daze, I met Elysa. What struck me most was her ambition. In as far as her personality was concerned, she won me over. She backed up her persona with a sophisticated style that said to the onlookers, "I'm about business. Knuckleheads need not bother!" She was super short, about 4' 11", and *really* pretty. During our first conversation, I found out that we'd attended the same college, and even had some mutual friends. When we talked, I always felt like a 'grown-up'. We talked a lot about fine restaurants, traveling, and building wealth – all topics of interest to me.

But, I could tell, Elysa was consumed by them. Our friendship grew, and soon, we became an item. We were together all day –every day. My bedroom escapades with Elysa taught me a valuable lesson: *never take a woman who can get an orgasm from good old fashioned penetration for granted.* They are few and far between! Elysa and I were a dynamic couple. She loved that I was an artist, and got behind everything I did professionally. Likewise, I had a healthy respect for her drive and entrepreneurial ambitions. However, I felt used in a way. Often times, it seemed as if she was really working solely for her own benefit. Still, her encouragement was nice. I started an Afro-centric T-shirt line. The shirts sold well, very well. The first time I was out, just 'doing me', and I saw a total stranger rocking' one of my joints, I was ecstatic. It's a feeling I still can't describe! I knew I wanted more. The T-shirt thing was cool, but I HATE DRIVING, and I really wasn't into all the running around. Pick-ups and drop-offs weren't my thing. Elysa's ambition must have rubbed off on me. I took some of the dough I made, and with the help of some investors, I opened up an urban- contemporary clothing store in a local mall. I called it Wear It's At! , It was my pride and joy! Ironically the store ended up being where *I* was from 9am until 10pm, EVERYDAY! But, I didn't mind. I knew I was onto something great. Very quickly, I had a loyal following. I had full-time employees, and was being wooed by vendors from all over the country! Wear it's At! was a SUCCESS! I was a success – *sort of.* . I decided that since the concept of Wear It's At! Was Hip –Hop, I would be true to the sub-culture that I had fallen for. Every Saturday we had freestyle ciphers, and rappers from all over the city came to show and prove! We also displayed the work of local graffiti artists, last but not least, the models! I felt like the store needed its own fly girls; I just hadn't found anyone who fit the bill. One night as me and my ace set up a party, she appeared through the crowd, this was a "grown folks" event, meaning 35 was the average age, but *she* looked my age. As the movie in my head turned to slow-mo, there she was. A long black dress delicately draped her pecan skin, her body, a prototype, from which a legion of the Amazon queens could be created. Her waist, so small, that I almost wondered if she ate at all, had its absence not brought attention to her taut, thick, muscular frame. As my gaze fixed itself on her face, I was frozen by her regal high cheek bones, whose contours led directly to her full, succulent red lips. Her hair was elegantly pulled back into a ponytail, (as if she knew how intoxicating the nape of her neck was) and the only jewelry she wore was the perfect complement to her appearance, it was her warm and inviting smile. I approached with a degree of trepidation, although I had pulled some cuties in my travels, never this captivating. If I didn't know me,

I would've thought the little voice in my head (James Earl Jones) was saying "she's waaay outta your league... SIT YO' ASS DOWN!" well, there was none of that happening, besides, I was already standing right in front of her... time remaining to say something clever and original. Approximately 2 seconds. Hmm a lot of guys have approached her tonight, this music is so 1978, these people's clothes are so out of date! GOT IT! "Oh my Gawd!" I gasped, "What's wrong? " She responded "I hate this job! They told me I had to pass out Ben-Gay and Geritol to the patrons! They're eating' this stuff like jelly beans!" she was laughing. I'M IN! I went on to say "do you know how many Crown Royal bags I've taken to the lost and found!?" By this time, I guess because I had this seriously distressed dumbass look on my face, she placed her hand on my shoulder as her laughter gently shifted to a sexy giggle. I said "seriously though, I think you are the most beautiful woman I've ever seen. But I don't have time to talk, because of my work with the elderly. But the way I made you smile, when I saw you, I felt like that inside... so here I am!" Apparently, the combination of stupidity and sweetness; made her curious. She grabbed my wrist and said "maybe you should be taking care of someone younger tonight?!" I turned to the crowd, and in my best Eddie Murphy voice I yelled "Leonard! …. Leonard! I QUIT!" when I turned back around and there she was, laughing again! "Well, looks like I have time for a dance!" I said, and so there I was trying to look cool and calm, while inside I was like YAAY ME! YAAY ME! We found a quiet place to talk in the lobby and she shared her story with me. She was from the west suburbs and only came in town to attend dance classes; her ambition was to be a professional dancer. That's when it hit me! "Would you be interested in dancing/modeling at my store on weekends after class?" "You have a store!?" she replied with elevated interest (this is the part where I smile and look right into the camera) so I proceeded to fill her in with the details. After about a month of "modeling" for me, we started to spend a lot of "down time" together. Our conversations had been usually over lunch; we'd walk to the food court and crack jokes as we stuffed our faces. The funny thing about having lunch with her was, she would insist on wearing the clothes I had given her to model! From an advertising standpoint, this was AWESOME! However, the flurry of smacks on the back of the heads that guys got (for staring at my gorgeous employee) was so constant that it almost sounded like applause! Once, after lunch as we walked back to the store, she asked if she could keep the outfit she was wearing. "Of course," I responded, "but, you have to tell people where you got it though!" As she smiled, and wrapped her arm around mine, she gave me as soft kiss on the cheek (this is the part where I become aware that I'm being played like a fiddle) and then she jumped in front of me and said "I really like you!" Surrounded by shoppers, I let my eyes convey my feelings, I reached out to gently place my hand on the back of her neck, and I pulled her close to me, kissed her, and then kissed her forehead.. as our eyes reconnected, I whispered" I like you too!" The rest of the work day was like being back in high school, sneaking smiles and sharing glances, even as she modeled in my storefront window, she would turn to look at me and smile. At the end of the day (as I closed the store down) she asked if she could change in the dressing room, instead of going to the ladies room. "Sure" I responded, and as she dipped away, I counted the take for the day, minutes later she called out "I think I need a hand!" "Okay, gimme a Sec" I said, when I got to the door of the dressing room, I asked what the problem was, to which she responded "whatever it is you can't help myself from out there" As I pulled back the curtain, there she stood, her body was like a tumultuous sea of caramel, my lust was the boat that navigated her mountainous waves. Her right arm attempted to cover her brown sugar breasts, as her hand rested on the nape of her neck, with her head tilted down slightly, her eyes smiled invitingly as she looked up at me. "I need more help than I thought!" she said softly. She released her bountiful bosom from their prior restraint as she grabbed my neck and pulled herself to me, her kiss was forceful, but tender. As I ran my hands down her silky legs that were still moist from her dance earlier, I grabbed her thigh right above the knee and pulled it up to my waist. Playtime was over! As our lips and tongues danced a kizomba, I grabbed her ponytail and pulled her head back, like a hungry vampire, I devoured her exposed neck, playfully licking and baby kissing a path back to her lips, stopping for a moment to nibble on her chin, as I caressed her like I had the hands of a blind man!. I was fully aware that this woman possessed the body of a goddess, and it was time to kneel before her. I began my show of adoration on her soft enticing thighs. Casually licking and kissing, as I made my way to her gift. I approached like her "wonder" was a bowl of soup… and when I got done making sure she was ready I eagerly sucked in her juices. I could feel her body begin to quiver, and as her moans got louder I paused, and stuck my finger in her waiting mouth to quiet things down. To my delight, she softly bit my fingers and then pulled them into her mouth harder and harder with each respectful lick I gave her; I plunged two fingers inside her and playfully tickled her. When her trembling seemed uncontrollable she grabbed my head and filled my wanting mouth with her enjoyment. As she rode my face into ecstasy we moved in unison like images in a mirror, I wanted her to know that I would dance with her until the music stopped. As she fell back to a chair she said "what are you trying to do to me" I smiled and held out my hand, as she grabbed it, I turned her around, she kneeled on the chair and turned to kiss my soul. As if to welcome me she wiped the sweat that dripped from my head and turned, as she used it to shine her truly magnificent ass. I entered slowly, like I was saying "can I have this dance?" and as the music in my head got louder my strokes got harder... while the bass line thumped, I found myself giving her my music, a mix between Jodeci and 9 inch nails. As I Softly ran my fingers across her brown velvet skin. I slowly moved in and out of her, and the next minute wrapping her ponytail around my wrist and pounding her pleasure with all of me. When I was ready; I jumped out and she bathed in my splash, and we laid there in the dressing room exhausted, we laughed and kissed each back to consciousness. Her stint with me didn't last long; as her dancing career skyrocketed. Apparently she had been discovered by a local up and coming R&B singer, who became so entranced by her that they married. The next time I saw her was difficult, she was on a reality show with a bunch of other jaded women, gone was the sweetness, the inner beauty the welcoming disposition. These qualities had disappeared. I don't know what that guy did to her... but I'm glad we had our moment in time.

A few months in, Elysa came by the store to visit. Although we didn't spend a lot of time together, as a matter of fact, we had reduced our dealings to the occasional "hook up" but; we still loved each other. She asked if I'd eaten, and since I was starving, we went up to the food court and grabbed a bite. That's when she dropped the bomb. Elysa was pregnant! I was super excited – although because of my regularly poised demeanor, nobody could tell. Now I really had to grind, and I only had 9 months to do it!

The pregnancy was rough. Elysa was put on bed rest, but even that wasn't helping. My 9 months turned into 6 and a half, and there he was. At just over 1 pound, my son was born! I had ditched my legal name a long time ago. Years earlier, my Mom shared the story about how I got my name. It seems that while she was still woozy from the medications given during childbirth, my father's mother wrote in the name that *SHE* wanted me to have. So, both in protest and out of respect for the woman who had sacrificed so much for my sister and me, I insisted everyone call me Gregg. And so, I gave my son the name my mother wanted for ME... Gregory. It meant more to me to give Mom that, than for me to have a junior. From now on, my Mom will be able to call out the name she had always wanted to. Now

my life had taken on a whole new meaning. I could no longer be concerned only with myself; my baby boy was in intensive care. So, every night, after I closed the store, I headed to the hospital and spent time looking at him – holding him learning (from the nurses) how to care for him. From the apnea monitor and the nebulizer treatments right down to wiping his little nose; I studied, each night for as long as I could. Then, I would shoot home; grab a quick nap head back to open the store. It was physically and emotionally draining, but my soul was replenished every time I held my little boy. This went on for a few months. Eventually he was released from the intensive care unit, which meant we were now on duty! , 24 -7. Meanwhile, my relationship with Elysa faded to nearly nothing.

I wanted to be a father; *and* a husband. I wanted my son to have what I had not. I didn't want him to be *deprived* of anything – an extremely selfish outlook. But the love Elysa and I shared was manufactured; it wasn't organic. It seemed honorable to me, at the time, but my hope that things would work out was because of my son – not for love. We decided to live together, and that's when shit got REAL. When she arrived home with my son, she was equipped with a huge air tank, an apnea monitor and a nebulizer – in addition to all the standard baby care stuff. My boy had still had tubes in him, *things* were very rough with him… but he was home.

Interactions with Elysa were strained at best. She wasn't all gung-ho entrepreneurial anymore. She was different! I suppose I was expecting the ideal situation, but it just didn't work. Here I was, bustin' my ass to keep the store thriving, only to come home and find out the Elysa had spent much time perfecting her Buppie skills. Her domestic skills were lacking, to put it mildly. There were dirty dishes, but no food was being cooked. When I got home at night, *I* had chores; which pissed me the fuck off! It wasn't long before we split up, and she moved out. It shook me though. Perhaps that's why I got a bit lackadaisical at the store.

Right after the holidays, I got into it with the management staff at the mall. I made so much dough over the holidays, that they wanted to change my lease, so that their cut was bigger – lot bigger. I refused, because my arrogance led me to believe that, since I had become a prime destination point, THEY couldn't do without me. I was wrong, and I lost the battle. Respect though, to all my supporters during that time who staged protests. Even the local news came out, but by that time, it was a wrap.

I was so broken. I just crawled under my proverbial rock and stayed there - for nearly a year!

When my son was two years old, he came to live with me. He stayed with me on and off, mostly on, until he was 17. Over the years Elysa became more and more difficult. We barely speak now. But, out of deference to my son, who may read this one day, I have left out the details that led to the way his parents feel about each other. After all, what's important is how we feel about HIM; and we are both immeasurably proud.

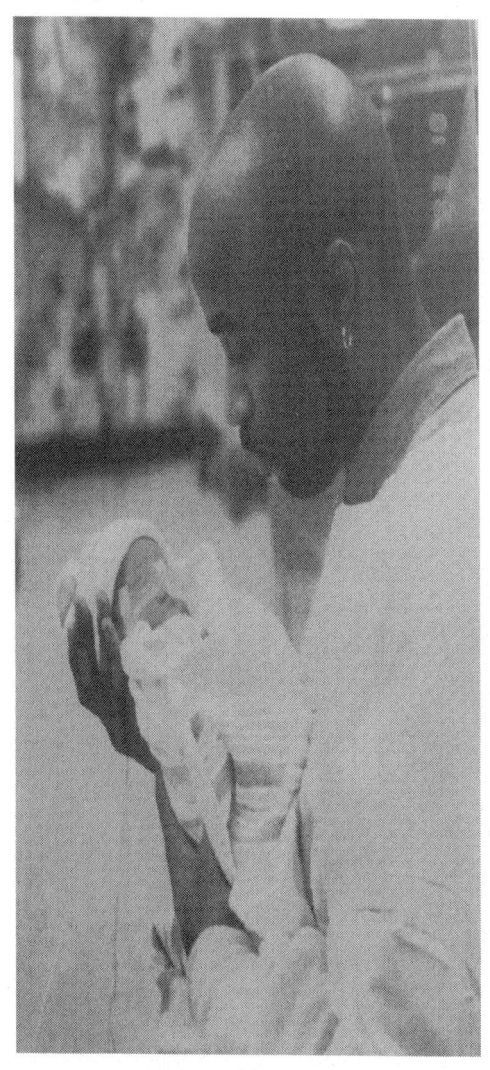

Hey DJ

I'm out from under my rock! I'm back from the dead! I'm partying again! By now, my best buddy had successfully climbed the local disc jockey ladder, and the functions we set-up were more upscale – better clientele, and better locations. It was extra cool. I got to hob-knob with tons of A-list celebrities, and play with Chicago's finest women. One night, we were at a private shindig in the west suburbs. As usual, I took the less aggressive approach with the ladies. My dude, on the other hand, was more of a head first kind of guy. From what I witnessed his style worked for him. But, my mentors taught me that being yourself was not only easier, it made you more appealing in the long run. So, whenever my dude would say something outlandish, I just laugh to myself, and watch women fall for it. I thought it was fascinating how all of these educated, professional, sisters could appreciate a guy who basically was, for all intense and purposes, obnoxious, rude, and full of himself. But I'll get to *that* story later.

Throughout the course of the evening, I stumbled into one of my dude's 'victims'. She had a short, Anita Baker-style haircut, big pretty eyes, and a beautiful smile. I had a CRUSH, and her name was DJ. She asked me if my friend was crazy. To which I replied, "Of course, but his doctor said that we should slowly introduce him to social situations to help his growth. Tonight we let him out with NO HELMET!" She thought that was funny, and we sat around and drank while the crowd seemed to disappear around us. Those eyes had me, but I was cool. DJ and I would talk on the phone for hours, every night. She was intelligent and funny; and after a while, she began referring to me as her *soul mate*.

But, I was involved with someone at the time. Truth be told, I was in the midst of a love triangle – Danni, Stacy, and ME. Danni was a dancer for a hugely successful Chicago native and popular R&B singer. Stacy was just *fine*; mixed race, extra thick, and super FREAKY!

Danni had the most elegant body that I'd ever seen – Prima Ballerina – she was graceful when she moved. Sometimes, I would watch her walk down the hallway and just smile.

One time, she looked back and caught me peeking. She giggled and asked me to come closer. I approached her, and I felt myself getting excited with every step. In the middle of my narrow hallway, we converged with a deep kiss. Danni wrapped her leg around my thigh and caressed the back of my neck. With the perfect synchronicity of a ballroom dance, we moved in unison. The hallway was our dance floor. We did a soulful Paso-doble from one end of the hall to the other. We couldn't stop. Every time she moved, to arch her back, point her toes, or bite my lip, I was overcome by the need to consume her visually and physically. One always fed the other, so I *always* wanted her.

We made our way to the dressing room, where I sat in my big chair and guided her to climb onto the arms. As she lowered her precious to my eager lips, Stacy came in, and didn't hesitate to join us. She put one hand on Danni's sweat-shined posterior and simultaneously ran the other through my chest hair. She walked around to kiss Danni, then bent down to kiss me softly, while I went back to give Danni's sunshine the attention it deserved. Stacy found that my joy was in need of attention, so she graciously treated me like a Popsicle on a hot, summer day.

As my excitement began to rise, she turned and placed me inside her. We all danced together. And when they knew I was ready, they knelt before me. We bathed each other, enjoyed a meal – that we all had a role in preparing – and adjourned to the bedroom. Life was GOOD! We were having a ball, doing everything together, and we all got along great!

As much as I enjoyed hanging with my girls, I told my soul mate that – when she asked me to – I'd be more than happy to drop their asses like hot potatoes! Eventually, she asked.

I called Stacy and Danni – and get this – I actually told them THE TRUTH! What's more, not only did they accept the news, they supported it! So much so, that I was inspired to call *all* the miscellaneous women in my Rolodex and tell them "It's a wrap!"

One of many calls was to Lana. Although we had had an otherworldly experience on the stairs, we *were* great friends. Still, I was so deep into DJ even Lana had to go.

I'm completely unencumbered now, and ready to become one with my "soul mate." I hadn't seen DJ since we met, partly because she lived in a far west suburb of Chicago, but mostly because I *hate* driving! Regardless, she couldn't take it anymore; so she drove into the city to see me.

When she stepped out of the car, I was DONE! I was ready to cash in my chips! She was drop-dead gorgeous! But more importantly, the loose jumpsuit she wore the night we met, had hidden her supremely thick girl physique! She was sporting a pair of skin-tight jeans, a spaghetti string top, and some sexy high-heels. Like Morris Day used to say, "Mary sweet mother Jesus!" This woman was FINE - big round hips, sumptuous booty, a perfect 36D cup, and pretty feet! As I said, I WAS DONE. You hear me!

We solidified our relationship after a series of long talks, and – since this is a tell all – I will say that our first interaction wasn't exactly a back breaker; at least not at first. We tried to talk, but we were both so full of anticipation that we found ourselves immersed in a passionate make-out session. It started with us gazing into each other's eyes and exploring each other's tongues until we were both about to pop. When she stood to undress, I was dumbfounded by her dimensions! It was like having my own personal dancer from a Luther Campbell video! Unfortunately, my *'self'* wasn't himself that night! Hey, we all suffer from performance anxiety occasionally. She was cool about it though, and after about twenty minutes, I was back to my good ole' back breaking *self!* She had gone to the kitchen to get something to drink, and just looking at her enough to 'activate the flow of excitement'.

I asked her to climb onto the kitchen countertop as I opened the refrigerator. I reached for the ice cream, and the strawberry topping, donned an impish grin, and said, "I hope you like ice cream!" Then I proceeded to make a mouthwatering DJ Sundae, right on top of her bubblicious goodness! I devoured my delicious dessert as she wiggled around the counter moaning, "Ooh-shit, ooh-shit." I thoroughly licked her clean, and then I took her by the hand and led her into the living room, where I carefully positioned her on the sofa so that her heart shaped ass was all I could see. I simply had to take a moment to enjoy her luscious derriere.

I started with her left cheek then moved slowly to the right... licking, sucking, nibbling, and probing as she moaned... sweetly. I stood back to admire her remarkable frame, giving her a moment to relax before turning her over so I could see the expression as I plunged back and forth inside of her. A seamless blend of pleasure and pain adorned her beautiful face, and when the time came, I erupted with a scream – all over her body. OH YES! Afterwards, as Jill Scott said, "We lay there sweaty, sex-funky – happy as we want to be."

DJ moved in, unofficially, which was odd because I didn't even have a job. But I managed; I was deeply in love! We went out a lot and doubled-dated with my best buddy who, by sheer coincidence had met a girl named La Tanya from the same suburb as DJ. Even crazier, they were friends! So here we all were, just kicking' it! Nobody could tell us anything.

We were young. We had an apartment, a Mustang – my buddy's – and, two of the finest women in Chicago! Perfect! But, *this* was what's commonly referred to as the calm before the storm.

First, the winds started to blow. I got home one day and hear people talking as I walked up the stairs to "our" apartment. That wasn't unusual, because DJ and my sister, who lived in the Apartment downstairs, had become fast friends. I put my things down and listened. I heard my name in their conversation. Now I'm REALLY listening. Much to my chagrin, they were talking about me – but not in a good way. It was a total "He ain't Shit Fest!" Yep, my sister and the *current* love of my life were having an in depth talk about how much I sucked. Well Naturally, I was on about FIFTY-THOUSAND After I'd heard enough, I almost kicked the door off the hinges. The look on their faces was pure surprise, guilt, and fear all wrapped into one. I kicked my sister out of the apartment, lit into DJ for engaging in the conversation, and promptly thanked her for saying "how she *really* felt." Then, I kicked her out! Now, I know I was broke, but I wasn't a jerk. I was a good brother to my sister, and the best man I could've possibly been to DJ. Well, okay, so I did kind of suck. Still, one of them should've either disengaged or defended me. But whatever!

After that, the relationship forecast was partly cloudy – indefinitely. DJ and I we're cool, but now that I knew she didn't respect me, we were both waiting for the first rain drop to fall.

The first of several scattered showers was at a family BBQ. I was on the grill. Everyone was having a good time until my sister requested a side bar. She asked me, "Since when did you start giving hickies?" To which I replied "Huh", and she said to me, "MAAAN, you didn't see those hickies on DJ's neck?!" I was done, and NOT in a good way. This was more of the "Why would you come here and embarrass me in front of my family?" kind of DONE!"

Lightning struck. Thunder roared. Raindrops were falling. Now, let the STORM commence.

My dude had moved in with his girl, La Tanya. Things were going fine; until the day I got a call from his *other* girl. She was a big time record company executive who my dude had been seeing for a couple of years. She'd been to our apartment too many times to count, and she was super cool. She and I were friends. His *other* girl asked me if I knew that he had a live in girlfriend (he had moved La Tanya in). My silent pause told her all she needed to know. All hell broke loose!

I talked to my dude and told him what happened. I advised him, NOT to move his girl out. I told him, "You love her and, if you explain, she'll ride with you!" Instead, he kept up the façade so that, when his girl returned home from her music industry convention – the business my dude was using her influence to break into – it would seem like no one lived there with him. His front would've worked, except that, in the meantime – unbeknownst to him – the two ladies had already spoken on the phone!

Aw man homey! His *real* love, La Tanya, left him because he lied. His industry girl left him *AND* had him blackballed. Now, instead rubbing elbows with the hottest artists of the time, and working the most *exclusive* parties, my man was spinning' records at kid's parties and shit! She even told the I.R.S. about his tax evasion! SHIT!

After the smoke cleared, my dude asked me to attend a meeting with some of the people involved in *his* scandal. He lured me in by saying "Somebody said YOU were trying' to fuck La Tanya!" I was FURIOUS! I have *NEVER* broken the sacred, unspoken rule of Man Code - don't mess with your dudes' girl. It sounds hypocritical coming from me, I know, particularly due to my dealings with married women. But, I didn't know *those* guys! I had never even flirted with La Tanya who. I considered a friend. And although she called and asked if she could come over, right after the shit hit the fan, I stiff armed the idea.

I should mention though, that once, while she was waiting for my dude to come home, La Tanya met my son and my mom. We all were just chilling. However, I couldn't help but notice motherly interaction she had with Gregory. Her warm persona, natural beauty – like that of Halle Berry – and keen sense of humor prompted my mother to ask a question as La Tanya left the room to play with

Gregory, "When are you getting married?!!" To which I replied "DJ and I aren't ready for that yet." She quickly smacked me on the back of the head and said, "FOOL! Your wife is playing with your son right now!" I knew what she meant, La Tanya and I did have a peanut butter to jelly type of vibe... but that was just our natural dynamic... There were no stolen moments or lustful stares ultimately; my buddy had met her first. Did we have a connection? Yes, but I *never* broke the code!

I knew when she called that she was trying to give me some vengeance coochie! And, even though she was incredibly good looking, and a truly good person, I simply said "NOPE". But NOW, I want to know the source of this misinformation. Outside of that exchange, La Tanya and I hadn't spoken at all.

When we get to the meeting, at a posh apartment overlooking Lake Shore Drive, I listened to everyone speak. Then I asked, "Who said I was trying' to hit La Tanya?!" It felt like I was looking around the room in slow motion. NOBODY knew what I was talking about! It was my dude! – My man, fifty grand – who thought *I* played him. We remained friends for a while, but I never got over that betrayal. That was the beginning of the end for us. DJ and I, however, pressed on amidst the storms.

It was funny, because I didn't take our rekindling as seriously as I should have. I was dismissive; although I'm pretty sure the psychological term is *denial*. Hickies aside, I loved me some Lady DJ!

Admittedly, the sex was mediocre. I recall one evening, on 69th Street, after dining alfresco, she asked "Did you like the head?" I looked at her and said, "You were giving me head!?" She was gorgeous, and despite the pesky little tidbits that kept popping up, I wanted to believe in her. In time, things evened out, and we were able to get back in a groove. Even though I was always attracted to her, the chemistry between us was lukewarm at best. It lacked PASSION! Despite our less than fervent attraction, we stepped our game up in the bedroom.

She had tricks and shit! *Finally*, she was listening to the requests I had been making. I was ecstatic! Little did I know, she was under Cutty's tutelage - circa Dead Presidents. On one occasion, DJ was in the bathroom with her birthday suit on, and what a suit it was. Her big juicy thighs, perfectly hung breasts, fully developed calves, and award winning a gluteus MAXIMUS were magnetic. I couldn't resist; and had little regard for the fact that she was still applying the baby oil. Like most guys, I imagine, I didn't give a damn about all her prep work. To me, it was like watching your vehicle exit out the car wash; I couldn't wait to jump it! What a session that was. We used every prop in the bathroom to assist with our pleasure, right down to spanking that magnificent ass with the back scrubber! Our sessions went on like that for a while, and I must say that, our little bathroom jaunt was the only time in my recent past that I hit it raw - pulling out in what I thought was the nick of time. Of course weeks later she said she was pregnant. Being the guy I am, despite my utter lack of finances, and the fact that I was having major problems with my son's mother, I fully embraced the newcomer. After, I did really love DJ. I could have been fulfilled having her as my wife and soul mate.

Of course, I was there for the prenatal visits; and at home, I waited on her hand and foot. As the "big day" got closer, I was full of anticipation! When that day finally did arrive, I was home, in Chicago, and she had gone to visit family in the west suburbs. My mother and I jumped in the car and set out there with the quickness! We arrived at the postcard worthy medical facility which was tucked in between big, beautiful trees and surrounded by an immaculately manicured landscape. The hospital staff so friendly, it was almost surreal! The big moment had come and gone. We had actually missed the delivery. But, I was relieved to know that both my love and my new baby boy were doing fine! I entered the recovery – which resembled a Holiday Inn suite – to see DJ lying there with the child, glowing. My mom was with me and we all gathered around to see the new addition to our families. When the time came for me to hold my baby boy, I was both nervous and excited. But, as usual, I managed to stay cool.

There he was... *my* boy? We named him Cameron. He was an awesome sight to see - dark skinned, curly hair, and a cute puffy nose. Yeah... no. This definitely was NOT *my* baby. To keep things cool, on the way home, I kept my thoughts to myself.

I didn't mention to my mom that, apart from the kid, not looking like either one of us, when I held him, I felt absolutely NO connection. There was no bond

A few days later, DJ said she wanted to "talk". I sat and listened, as she went on about the baby being fathered by her ex-boyfriend. Poncho, according to her, he had no job, six kids, and three waiting – including DJ's – with four different 'baby mamas'. Strangely enough, I was so deeply in love with DJ I suggested I raise Cam as my own. But, she declined. Ultimately, the self-imposed shame was too much for her, and soon after, we lost touch.

I found out later that she had moved to Atlanta. One day, while browsing on social network – which I rarely do – there was a message from DJ "I've been looking for you," she wrote. She left her number, so I called. She said Cam was doing fine and that, barring her current relationship, life was good. Once again, she managed to get involved with a guy that had multiple kids and heavy baggage. I did the best I could to counsel her. We spoke every few months or so. During one conversation mentioned that she'd be in town, and that she would love to see me. I was cool with that. After all, it had been nearly seven years since I'd laid eyes on her. We met downtown, but the car she borrowed was ready to give out. So, instead of the dinner date I planned, we slowly made it back to my place. I must say, she looked even *better* than I remembered. The years had been *very* kind to her.

When we arrived at my place, she was amazed at how I had transformed the apartment. Surely having *real* furniture and no candy wrappers on the floor was a marked improvement. We ate, and we talked. The rest of the night consisted of an exclusive tour of the apartment. We went from one room to the next, doing nasty things to each other all… night… long.

There were constant messaging alerts and ringtones from her phone, and in the middle of our sex tour, she felt the need to explain that since her phone wouldn't roam, she had borrowed that phone from a "friend". I'm like "Whatever," I thought, "let's get back to business!" We did. The 'tour' culminated with a 5-star fellatio routine that included a prayerful incantation, "C'mon… C'mon," she chanted, as she alternated strokes. Of course, I did. My energy was released everywhere – more specifically, over the phone that she borrowed from her 'friend'. We laughed. It was funny.

As we lay together, ready to fall asleep, I couldn't help but think to myself, "I love you. DJ. You're beautiful, but after all this time, you still ain't shit!" To keep it real though, I would *definitely* do her again. But, *never* would I take her seriously, or lend her my phone!

Ready Or Not?

My best bud had been around for about ten years. Our relationship had survived a total shit-storm, and we were back to our old tricks. Most of the time we just hung out, like guys do, either looking for girls or talking about girls. Maybe we would squeeze in some work. We were young. Our main focus was FUN!!! Naturally, when my dude got weekly bookings at one of Chicago's premier night clubs, I was stoked, as you can probably imagine. As I said, we were young, but we knew how to fake maturity. So even though clubs were for the 30 and older crowd, we used our player training to its maximum capacity! The entire staff was in our pockets. Everyone, from the photographer to the coat checker, was willing send women to the D.J. booth for their favorite "lil" guys. I met dozens of women, including a lifelong friend, Trisha – who happens to be gorgeous!

Meeting her was when I began to develop a fondness for "extreme" women. One night at the club, I spotted Trisha. She had the most unbelievable dimensions I've seen; and she still does! True, I'd had my share of curvaceous beauties. But Trisha was different. She was SPECTACULAR! Let me create a visual. Trisha measured 38 TRIPLE *I*, with a 30" waist, and 42 inches at the hips. Trisha and I talked quite a bit. We had plenty in common, including a love of poetry and similar musical tastes. We would even share our favorite songs over the telephone. We grew very close, and she visited occasionally. Our quality time was incredible. Soft music played in the background while we engaged in conversation - sharing our goals and dreams. I was so into *her* that I didn't see her as a sexual takedown. She was the object of my *metaphysical* desires.

On the outset this seemed like the perfect union, then one day I called, as I had done many times before, only to get cursed out! "Don't any Trisha live here!" the lady's screamed. Well, okay. I presumed that she re-connected with her old boyfriend or something. Or, maybe there was something I didn't know. What I *do* know, is that one night when I got home from work, my guys were outside waiting. They rushed me, asking "Who was ol' girl?" I didn't know who they were talking about. But, they went on to describe a woman with eye-popping proportions, wearing a seductive, black, lace dress. Someone had stopped by, rang the doorbell, waited for a while, then left. Since I was single... that could have been at least four of my new "friends" or maybe it was... TRISHA! I tried again to make contact. This time, a guy cursed me out! FUCK... FOR REAL!? Many years passed. Trisha was all a distant memory, albeit a pleasant one.

Some years later, I was pressured to attend to attend a party at a local Jamaican nightclub. I walked in, and through the crowd, there she was – just I remembered. Trisha stood there, donning a pair of white shorts that showcased her thick, well-defined legs. She wore a matching white top, and a lacy shawl to camouflage her *extremities*.

With a mixture of anticipation and anxiety, I made my approach. What if she didn't remember me? As I got closer, she turned and looked my way. "Do you remember me?" I asked. Trisha giggled, and smiled so bright it lit up the night's sky. "Of course I do Gregg!! I'm so happy to see you," she answered excitedly. We sat down to talk.

Trisha explained that, because of her situation at home, she had enlisted in the National Guard. She said that, during her stint in the service she thought about 'us often. I felt a great sense of relief. We were delighted that fate had brought us back together.

A couple of days later, Trisha called. She asked if I'd like to come by her place for a cocktail. I thought back on the conversation we had at the club, where she mentioned that she was practicing a celibate lifestyle. (EWWW!) Being the sexual creature that I am, I was a little apprehensive. It would be challenging to be around this *gorgeous* woman and just… talk. I followed my instincts and let the shallow – *male* side of my brain prevail. I responded to her invitation the best way I knew how, saying, "I'll let you know in a few, 'cause I don't think can find a babysitter." That was a total LIE. My son was spending the weekend with his mom!

Anyway, she said that she understood and she REALLY hoped I could make it! As I relaxed and prepared to call her back with the 'bad news', I received a text that reads "I hope you can come!" Attached, was a picture of Trisha. She was wearing a red, lace teddy and a pair of 4 inch, platform heels, and her smooth, chocolate skin was glistening from the baby oil.

I dialed her number and slipped on some pants. I was calling to tell her that, magically, I had found a babysitter. The phone barely rang when she picked up and laughed. "I guess you got my picture," she said. "YES I DID!" I quickly responded. Trisha seemed happy that I was able to find a sitter – at least she said she was – and she promised to keep the outfit on until I arrived. By the time she finished talking, I was in the car and on my way – not that I was eager. I may have run a few red lights and jumped a few curbs in my haste, but nobody got hurt - except for that old man in the wheelchair, but he landed in the grass... I think.

I told Trisha that I would give her a call when I got close. I did – she didn't answer. Immediately, I was tailspin because of what happened with her in the past. I called again... then again... nothing. So, I went back home. No sooner than I pulled into my parking space, my phone rang. "Hey baby." she said to me, "I see you called. I was in the kitchen making something to eat, are you close?" I told her that I'd gone back home, since she didn't answer, and suggested we connect another time.

"I understand," she said. And, that was that. Moments later, I received another text – a picture her voluminous breasts, drenched with candied yam sauce – my favorite. The caption reads, "I spilled some candied yams!" Naturally, I called to say I was back on the road. This time, she answered the door. Trisha was still wearing the sexy, red teddy, but she had cleaned the yam sauce off, thinking I would lick, umm *like*, it better fresh. She was right! She welcomed me into her home and asked if I would I like a drink. I asked for a Scotch – on the rocks. She served a scrumptious soul food meal: roast beef, macaroni and cheese, candied yams, and greens. It was fantastic; great meal is quite an aphrodisiac!

We joked around for a while, and flirted with each other. The anticipation was building. Eventually, Trisha got up clear the table and asked I had room for dessert. Absolutely! She returned from the kitchen and her top had mysteriously fallen off.

Gingerly, she walked toward me, careful to balance the strawberries and whipped cream she had placed atop her bountiful bosom. Dessert was served. I licked the cream off of her chocolate saucers and consumed one of the red, ripe strawberries. My face was deeply immersed in her soft pillows, so I used the motion of devouring my berry to our advantage. My tongue and lips soon found her swollen chocolate drops – a perfect complement to the delicious fruit that Trisha had so graciously served. I took a second strawberry in mouth and offered her the other end. Our lips met. The electricity flowed through me. I stood up and gently glided my hands over her curves until I held her face in my hands. Our kiss was intense. Our souls touched.

In the back of my mind, I knew that sex was out of the question. And with that, I also knew that a trip downtown was inevitable. I took my time. All that body required my full, undivided attention!

I sucked each of her tiny toes – then-tickled the arch of her foot with my tongue. Trisha's perfectly sculpted legs were silky- smooth. I let my mouth explore, starting at her ankle, and traveling up her calves to picture-perfect thighs. Her brown skin shimmered in the soft light. I continued my journey, drawing circles up her spine with the tip of my tongue. She cooed as I reached the nape of her neck and began to nibble, tenderly, pulling her earlobes into my mouth. I motioned her to turn over, and I worked my way south. She was delicious, especially because I had brought a small cup of yam juice with me. My mission now, was to find what pleased her plum.

My voyage began with slow circles, round and round, and round. Then, stroking up and down, I painted her petals like an artist. Her body, writhing in satisfaction, whispered to me as she moaned. I had discovered a level of pleasure she had never known. I was fixated, intent on elevating her joy - massaging her love with my warm, moist tongue – flicking, tickling, teasing - making her thick legs tremble. She grabbed my head and pressed me into her sweetness. Her legs locked, and my mission was complete.

Though my reward was in achieving something many could not, Trisha wanted to return the favor. She sat me down and said, "I have something *else* for you." Kneeling in front of me, she surrounded my nature with her massive orbs, pouring baby oil in between them. My staff disappeared and then reappeared like a sailboat in a storm. The rhythmic heat and plush softness of her mounds created a euphoric sensation. I erupted with a great force. She looked into my eyes and said, "Now we've both had dessert!"

The next week Trisha called and said she wanted to stop by which, was always fine with me. When she arrived, she handed me a manila envelope and me to open it. "What is this?" I wondered. It was a poem, a14-page homage to my tongue! I was honored. And what better way to say thank you than to take her upstairs for a treat!

We continued to see each other, on and off, for about a year. Inevitably the question was asked, "So, what are we doing?" Translation: *Are we going be a couple, or not?* I shot off the obligatory, "Wha'd'ya mean," while I carefully crafted my reply. See, I had heard that she was involved with a Jamaican fat-cat who bankrolled a lot of her recreational activities. *That*, in conjunction with her hectic dating schedule, led me to what I thought was a rational conclusion. So I told her, there was no way I could keep up with her lifestyle, and that LOVE would probably *not* sustain us. My response garnered a less than lukewarm reception. Trisha vehemently disagreed. I assured her that sitting at home and going to see an occasional movie would eventually get old – she conceded my point.

I look at Trisha as a close friend, one who I can count on. However, this a perfect example of me getting the "green light" but stopping the car, while I sit there wondering why and the people around me honk their proverbial horns, as if to say WHAT THE FUCK IS WRONG WITH YOU?! I'm sure she feels the same. I still get a "Happy Friday" text every once in a while. I can't help but wonder sometimes, whether I should have given *us* a fair shot. On the other hand, there *are* only two continents; she hasn't been to, so maybe when she's done, we'll explore our own world!

The Elle Train

At twenty-seven I was doing great! Now with success comes sometimes notoriety, which I had achieved because of my store... I've learned, through the years, that some women find black men more appealing if they have "things". Don't misunderstand. I'm not talking about material "things," I mean other "things" – ambition, confidence, and self-esteem. Imagine that!

My partner and I had the mall on lock. We sponsored freestyle battles on the weekends, and of course there were the live models dancing in the display windows. During the week, when it got slow, I'd tend to the paperwork, balance the accounts, or draw to pass the time. Elle walked in. I remember it like it was yesterday.

She was PERFECT: short stature, classic style, big brown eyes, round hips, flawless breasts, and a lovely smile. She had come in with a friend of hers, and we engaged in casual conversation. By this time, my "game" had taken on a life of its own. So our conversation, although general, was all about subtext. As we looked into each other's eyes, talked, and smiled. She discreetly grabbed a pen from the counter, wrote her phone number, and slid it to me without missing a beat. I put it my chest pocket with the same discretion, and though she never *said* call me, her eyes did. Here was a woman with a different way of doing things, and she's gorgeous too!

So we talked regularly, and became quite friendly. The problem was that she was off at college, and lived 600 miles away. Even though she was super-cool, the distance was just too much! We lost touch, and that was that – or so I thought.

I left the retail business to pursue other interests. I had developed an arts curriculum and sold it to the local public schools. I piloted the program at my mother's school, and I was having a ball. One day, my mom asked me if I knew an Elle Townsend. It caught me by surprise, because I hadn't seen or heard from Elle in years. I told mom, I had known her briefly, and inquired as to why she asked. It turns out that my mom had interviewed her for a teaching position. Wow, REALLY?!

On Elle's first day, I popped in to say hello. It was like no time had passed. We picked up right where we'd left off. We talked on the phone constantly and everything! Elle invited me to attend a number of different events and, while we got pretty close, our relationship was platonic. Flirtatious, but – no –nookie! I had become a *friend*, and that was fine. We looked good together though, and we always had a ball.

During one of our chats, Elle suggested that *we* needed a vacation. "We deserved it", she claimed, and after giving some to the matter, I agreed. So, we booked a week-long trip to Puerto Vallarta, Mexico. I wanted my "friend" to fully enjoy her vacation, so when it came to getting to the airport, I took the liberty of hiring a limo – instead of riding there in the backseat of her friends car. I *am* a gentleman after all. Somehow, my use of the word shuttle vs *limo* pissed her off. I didn't understand it. I was only trying to surprise her. How silly of me! My kind gesture landed me in the hot seat, and we ended up having a rather heated discussion, the origins of which I still that I still don't know.

Eventually, she agreed to take the LIMO, and everything was cool. On the day of the trip, the driver arrived to pick her up. He even carried her luggage from her apartment door – just the kind of service I'd been looking for! Elle wasn't really impressed; either that or she simply refused to admit that the limo was a great idea! Since I knew *I* was right, I really didn't care what she thought. And, my next trick would be undeniable! What better way to defuse Elle's semi-funky attitude than to surprise her with one Chicago's of the finest hoagies and an oversized cookie for dessert? For whatever it was worth, I really wanted her to feel a little pampered. She didn't want the sandwich though – SHEESH!!

We arrived in sunny Puerto Vallarta. It was as if we'd traveled back in time and landed in the 70's. Who knew they still rolled the *stairs* out on the tarmac and up to planes, but whatever. We checked into the hotel, and headed out to the city. The night life was different, but fun. The clubs were gaudy and the music – well, let's just say I was GLAD when they played *Bust A Move*. Elle and I made the most of it, and had a great time. Later that night, back at the hotel, Elle crashed out. I sat on the balcony gazing at the moon and listening to the ocean, wishing she was awake to enjoy it with me.

Morning dawned and we hit the ground running. We ate breakfast, worked out, and then went to the lobby to choose the day's adventures. We listened as the representative explained each excursion, watching each other's facial expressions to pin a mutual interest. I was totally relaxed, sipping a drink laying back in my chair, with my sun glasses on, just CHILLIN'. When the tour rep finished her presentation, I sat up and thanked her, asking for a few minutes to make our decision. As SOON as the agent walked away, lovely travel partner yelled, "Why you got to be so DAMN nonchalant!" LUCIFER himself must have risen from the depths of hell to take over her spirit – there's no other explanation. Yep, she was possessed. I almost spit out my drink! I'd been thoughtful and attentive, a complete gentleman. The way I'd been doting over her, I people thought we were newlyweds. I responded by saying, "Baby, I was listening. All the trips sound cool, so I was just rolling with the lady's choice."

Thankfully, the tour rep returned quickly. Maybe the woman was ordained; maybe she had on a garlic necklace – I didn't care which. Elle's demon was vanquished. She went from shooting daggers from her eyes and spitting fire to grinning cheerfully from ear to ear. Elle looked at the representative and calmly said, "We'll take the day cruise."

I could hear my soul crying out, "Get another room! You can have fun by yourself!" Naturally, I ignored that little voice inside. I had love for Elle. She was just a little *edgy*, I thought.

We enjoyed the cruise, and Elle mellowed out a bit. We made our way back to town, walking… and walked… and walking. It was so fucking hot! "I KNOW WHAT'LL COOL ME DOWN," I thought to myself. WET WIPES! I had some in my backpack – *I was proud of myself for being so thoroughly prepared.* I wiped the sweat from my bald head, and I didn't even smell my alcohol covered skin FRYING in the hot Mexico sun. I was trying to cool myself, not cook myself. My brilliance had been thwarted by its ever-present rival – sheer stupidity! I marched on, deep-fried scalp and all, not letting the huge flakes of skin that were blowing off my dome deter me.

Finally, we were back for lunch. Keep in mind; this was an all-inclusive vacation, meals, drinks, the whole nine. We ate chicken wings and salad – keeping it light because our day trip included dinner.

Elle began to tell me how handsome, she thought I was, and express how much she appreciated all my efforts, saying that she "couldn't have picked a better travel partner. NOW that was what I'd been waiting to hear, but the "travel partner" bit let me know that sex was going NOT going to happen. Still, I relished her praise because, again, I loved her. She excused herself from the table and went to the ladies room. I felt good, and thought, "Now, we could just relax, and maybe even have some romantic moments." My daydream was interrupted when our waiter asked "Are you all finished?" "Oh yes… si… Gracias Amigo," I smiled.

Elle returned, with a different vibe. LUCIFER was must have been waiting to reclaim her soul and flushed it down the toilet!! "WHERE THE FUCK IS

MY CHICKEN!" hollered. All I could muster was a dumbass look and a "What?" She yelled again, "WHERE-THE-FUCK-IS-MY-CHICKEN!?" I explained that, since only a *tiny* piece of chicken wing had been sitting on her plate for the last 30 minutes, I let the waiter clear the table.

Elle went HAM! She cursed me out in front of our fellow vacationers, and stomped away. I stood up and called after her, as cool as possible, "Baby, you know this is *all you can eat* right? I'll just get you another plate." "FUCK YOU," she bellowed, from the mouth in the back of her neck. Really? Fuck *me*? Needless to say, the rest of the day wasn't a whole heck-of-a-lot better. We didn't speak at all – it was almost surreal.

Between the eruptions, we managed to have a pretty good time. There was a genuine level of care that Elle showed, especially when my "waterproof " wallet failed me, drenching all of my travelers' checks, she didn't hesitate to take on things until I got the matter taken care of. We got massages on the beach, bought a lot of jewelry, and partied – hard. Everyone knew us as 'the party couple'.

Later, I was on a boogie-board, *pretending* to have fun – acting like I was unaffected by Elle's increasingly high BITCH factor. But, I was really fucked up. I knew *I* didn't deserve to be the target of those eruptions, and started to wonder how long I could keep my game face. There were three whole days left before we'd be headed home. The *illest* shit of all was that, while I was "kicking' it" with my new friend – the boogie board – I spotted Elle out on the water clutching *Jorge* on the back of his jet ski! I can still remember how I felt... STUPID!!

I put my boogie board down and headed back to the room to change. With about 30 minutes before the boat would leave, I had plenty of time. I got to the room and knocked on the door. I could hear her in there. The music was loud, and shit was rustling around while I stood outside knocking. "I'll be out in a minute!" she yelled. Ten minutes later, and I was knocking. A bellboy walked by and asked, "Do you need another key, Senor?" "No," I replied, "I need a NEW WIFE!" We laughed and I went back to my humiliating wait. Finally, Elle snatched the door open and out she walked. She'd already showered and changed clothes. "See you later!" she said as she walked by, leaving me to catch the door before it closed. At this point, I there was little time left to make the cruise. I'm tripping, pissed off and beyond confused, but still going to this fucking $75 cruise. I grabbed the Corona T-shirt I won at a karaoke contest, washed my face and rolled out!

Just like in the fucking movies, I was literally running through the cobblestone streets of Puerto Vallarta asking the locals, "Donde esta Puerto?" As I ran up, the boat was pulling off. The party people were shouting, "C'MON JUMP!" Like Tom Cruise's character said in <u>Risky Business</u> "Sometimes you just got to say... what the fuck," I thought. I jumped. And I made it onto the boat and was welcomed with a drink and plenty of pats on the back. From the corner of my eye, I saw Elle. She approached me. No longer the Evil-Bitch-Demon Elle, she was now the smiling, shapely, sexy, apologetic Elle. "I'm sorry for my attitude earlier", she said, "Can we just have fun?" Well, I had no intentions of saying SHIT to her, but I thought, "Fuck it, why not!"

We were in full party mode – *samba line, tequila, body shots, and our version of the fucking Lambada* – we got it all in!! We finally reached the island. It was uncultivated, completely undisturbed, and amazingly beautiful. There was no sidewalk; just a beaten path that I knew would be difficult for Elle to manage wearing those high- heeled shoes. I took her hand, and with me as her crutch, we made it atop the mountain to a fantastic restaurant.

Unfortunately, with every step she took, Elle felt the effects of the shots we drank on the cruise. By the time we found a comfortable spot, she passed the fuck out. So I sat there at a dimly lit, romantic Mexican haven with an extravagant meal, and incredible view of the ocean, and a drunken bitch.

I figured four delightful things out of five weren't all bad, so I may as well enjoy! I made sure Elle as comfortable while I exchanged pleasantries with our fellow vacationers. I answered the obvious questions, "Is your wife okay?" and ""How's your wife?" And I was having a good time until, SHE arose - *cue scary music*!

I sat her up and asked if she wanted to eat; I'd taken the liberty of ordering her dinner. Starving, she said yes. Elle kept dropping her fork, so I offered some assistance; *I fed her* – so what! It was either make the most of a bad situation, or become a victim of one. She was feeling better after she ate, and announced that it was "time to tinkle". Much to my chagrin, I the waiter informed us that the outhouse style restroom was halfway down the mountain. Since Elle refused to take off her heels, and I it was dark, I escorted her to the bathroom. On the way down, we were stopped by a couple that we'd met, and partied with, on the mainland. The guy asked Elle if she was feeling okay, and in response, she hurled all over their shoes– YUK!

When we got to the outhouse, I stopped and told her I'd wait for her at the foot of the hill. She walked to the freestanding commode, looked back, and said "Don't PEEK, Don't PEEK! Was she being serious? What was there to see, a half drunken, vomit covered, delusional Queen Bitch sitting on a toilet surrounded by dirt, and bugs and shit? Elle must have thought I was the thirstiest man alive. "Don't peek – what an absurd statement," I thought to myself, and *somehow* managed to control the urge she thought I had to see half an ass cheek.

We made our way to the "natural' amphitheater. It was time for the show. The locals would perform historic, cultural dances. Two minutes after we sat down, torrential rain began to pour. The show was cancelled. Since we had no umbrella, I took off my shirt and placed it over Elle's head. We began our descent. This time, I insisted she take off those damned high-heels.

Aboard the boat, a curtain separated the front end from the back. The back of the boat was where all the hardcore partiers hung out. I pulled the curtain to the side and the crowd roared, "YAAAY!!" I used my free hand to give them all the "Ain't shit happening sign". The *party couple* was down for the count for the entire 40 minute ride back to Puerto Vallarta Elle slept in my lap... and I chilled.

After a long, incredibly dramatic, day we docked at Puerto Vallarta, where I was happy to find that Elle was less like a sleeping princess and more like just a passed out drunk. *Great!* No cabs or shuttles were available, since it was only three blocks from the docks to the hotel. *Fantastic!* A tranquil walk along the cobblestone streets of Puerto Vallarta, carrying 150 lbs. of dead fucking weight, was a perfect end to my cruise.

When we got to the room, I plopped her down on the bed, fell onto my own *separate* bed, and just fucking exhaled. My relaxed body and mind were rudely interrupted by the indelicate, rasping that only a person who had vomited repeatedly could deliver. "I'm hungry can you get me something to eat please?" Elle muttered. "Okay, baby," I replied, knowing good and well the kitchen closed 10 minutes ago. But, fuck it. Why let a technicality like that stop me – right? I went out to the restaurant and politely tapped on the door. A man answered; he'd been mopping the floor. Maybe he felt my pain, maybe he recognized the frustration on my face, or maybe he was just tired of mopping and wanted to take a break. Whatever the reason, he *sold* me the most expensive non-gourmet soup ever – mucho pesos! Mission accomplished! I returned to my sick, drunken, bitch of a princess, and fed her the soup as she lay in bed. Elle reward my heroism when she looked up at me with those big, brown, bloodshot eyes and said, "Did you remember to get salt?"

WHAT A BITCH!!!!

Well, except for the fact that I caught Montezuma's Revenge the next day and slept in the fetal position during the whole flight home, *and* had to take five more days off work to recuperate, I'd say the vacation went pretty well. And by that, I mean it was totally FUCKED UP!

A week or two after returning home from Puerto Vallarta, since we didn't have to share space, we were back bosom buddies. Everything was cool. While talking on the phone one day Elle said to me, "You know, my friends keep asking me 'wassup wit y'all?' and saying' " y'all are perfect together." She continued, "I thought about it, and everything I've been looking for has been right under my nose the whole time, so why don't we just do us?" Even though my brain said, "FUCK THAT," I heard "You know, that sounds real good baby… real good," come flying out of my mouth.

Later that week, under the glow of moonlight, as the music played softly in the background, I proposed. Elle said yes. Yes, dreams do come true! I had a beautiful fiancée, a promising career, and infinitely high hopes. Elle and I started spending more time together and we enjoyed each other's company. She even baked me brownies – my favorite dessert – which she brought by personally.

I was amazed, and somewhat startled, to really get into the mindset of marriage. We worked together and cared for each other. We loved each other.

Even though I wanted to stay home and eat brownies, we had business downtown. This time, when I say *we*, I mean my lovely, sexy significant other and me. After handling *our* business, I wanted to treat my lady to lunch. I took her to my favorite bistro, just off Chicago's Magnificent Mile. After a light meal, I wanted dessert. I decided to share my favorite dessert - again, brownies – with my lady. These brownies were exceptional! They were just the right consistency with chocolate chips inside, and sugar-coated bottoms – HEAVEN! As I ordered our delicious treats, I started to feel some heat radiating from Elle's body. I turned around; she was seething. "BROWNIES!" She yelled, "Why the FUCK would you order some FUCKING brownies?! *MINE* wasn't good enough?? Well, you DON'T have to worry! I WON'T MAKE YOU SHIT ELSE!!" She finished her rant and stormed out, headed toward Michigan Avenue – presumably to catch a cab home.

Even though felt thoroughly embarrassed, and humiliated, *and* didn't get any brownies, I followed her out. I begged her to let me take her home. I even promised not to speak. She finally caved and I took her home. Elle channeled the energy she'd saved while not speaking, into slamming the passenger door so hard that my door damn near flew open. Good times! After things died down, she called and apologized for over-reacting. I accepted.

Several weeks had passed since we had informed our loves ones about our engagement. The wedding plans had commenced, and our families seemed to be very happy about our union. Elle stopped by my place one morning, and since I wasn't used to AM visits from her, it was a pleasant surprise. She was having car trouble, the main problem being that her car was a rusted piece of shit! I temporarily fixed the problem, and casually mentioned that *we* needed to look at getting her some new wheels.

Even though we were engaged, we hadn't shared *any* intimacy. Don't trip. Sex doesn't always have to be the guy's motivation. Does it? Before Elle in the car, I tried to kiss her goodbye. She turned her head to the side and said, "I'm not ready for that. It's awkward – like kissing my brother!" I laughed it off and replied, "You be kissing your brother?!!" I didn't make a big deal of it.

Elle called the following weekend. She has a surprise for me, and asked me to stop by. Now this time, I *was* thinking sex – after all baked goods were out of the question. I arrived and she greeted me with a hug and kiss, on the lips. She invited me in and asked me to have a seat. I did, taking in the ambience. The smell of incense and her sweet perfume lingered in the air. And there was something else ... cookies?

Yes!" "I thought to myself, "I'm back in; I've been forgiven!" The brownie fiasco was a thing of the past, and Elle was about to extend a delicious olive branch.

Elle smiled and handed me the warm chocolate chip cookies. There was a note that read, and I'm paraphrasing, "If you didn't define yourself for yourself, you'd be crunched into other people's fantasies of you..." - Audrey Lord. My mind couldn't fire off enough synapses to figure out what that meant, I was confused. So I asked Elle to elaborate. She explained that she couldn't handle the pressure. She was calling off the wedding, but hoped we could remain friends. Just like the brownies, those cookies weren't as sweet as they should've been. And they left a bad taste in my mouth... as did the one who made them.

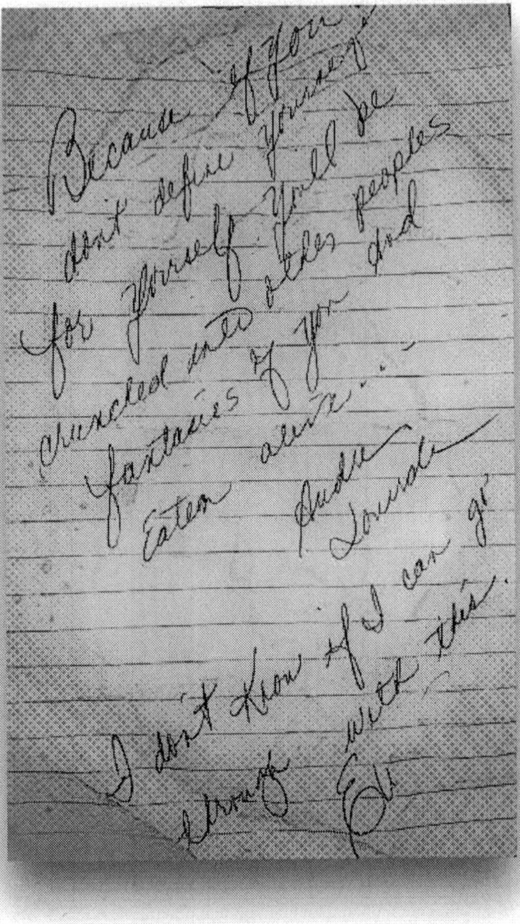

Because if you
don't define yourself
for yourself you'll be
crunched into other peoples
fantasies of you and
Eaten alive...

Audre Lourde

I don't know if I can go
wrong with this.

Ed

Just like Candi

It took me a year to get my mind right after Elle. I spent a lot of that time becoming a better man. I reflected on my experiences, and sifted through the bullshit to find some rationale and pinpoint my own accountability. I exploited the fact that I had more time than money and just thought about shit. *This is commonly referred to as being in a rut.* I was a social recluse, except for conversations with close friends. It simply wasn't time to return to the dating scene.

Summer rolled around, and my wounds began to heal. I had reached the point where I had forgotten why I'd been so fucked up emotionally. Both my sister and my mother were involved solid, progressive relationships. I saw that, and I was happy for them; they are amazing women who deserve to be cherished. It was time for annual vacation planning to begin. This summer, they wanted to rent some condos in Wisconsin and stay for about a week. I didn't have that kind of time, so they vigorously persuaded me. But, I refused; not because of the time, because of the *fifth* wheel factor. Why would I want to hang out with two couples for a whole week? That's damn near emotional suicide!

As usual, refusing my family's offer to join them for their little summer jaunt, led them to sponsor another familiar trip – a GUILT TRIP! My sister sat me down and said that her longtime friend had been going through some stuff and that she too was in need of a vacation. She suggested that, we could just share a condo. Candi and I had known each other for years, by default. In our youth, the 5 year difference in our age made for what could only be categorized as "Awww, that's so cute! She has a crush on me." However, Candi had grown into an attractive woman. She had desert brown skin, almond-shaped eyes, and straight, jet-black hairs. She definitely had a unique look. We had always enjoyed each other's company before, so I said, "What the heck." Candi was cool so fuck it. I wouldn't be a fifth wheel, and neither would she.

The thought of vacationing in Wisconsin held NO interest for me. In my opinion, "The Dells" was SUPER CORNY!! The cheesy hotels - if you'll excuse the pun - and pointless novelty shops were less than appealing. I was quite dismissive of the whole idea. I was pleasantly surprised, when we got there. There we all were – two couples, Candi, and ME – each "couple" with very nice lakefront condo of their own.

Things were cool. The first night, we all convened for dinner, conversation and board games. We had a lot of laughs. Candi had always gotten a kick out of my sense of humor, not that she thought I was funny necessarily; she was amused more in the, "Wow, did you really say that," kind of way. Eventually, we called it a night. Candi and I adjourned to our little condo. I slept on the couch, as any gentleman would, and she slept in the bedroom.

The main event for the next day was the Water Park. It had been so long since I have been down a waterslide that I'd forgotten how much fun it was! The more I got into it, the more I started checking my form – pointing my toes so I'd be more aerodynamic, and shit! I thought to myself, "If they make this an Olympic event, I'm gonna bring home the gold!" We all had a BLAST! The day ended with a lakefront barbecue and good conversation. My exchange with Candi was anything but flirty. I wasn't attracted to her. Well, I *was*, but I had it in my head that any relationship with her would be purely platonic. After all, what good could I possibly derive from dating my sister's BFF? NUTHIN! So, I stepped into the "friend" box.

By the time we returned to our condo, we'd gotten much more comfortable with one another. Since it was early, we decided to watch a movie, which quickly evolved into a sarcastic joking, storytelling extravaganza! I was on a roll; and so was Candi. We talked and laughed well into the night.

Over the course of the night, the couch seemed to get smaller and smaller. Soon, we were face to face, looking right into each other's eyes and we found ourselves locked in a kiss – long, deep, passionate, kiss. Candi whispered' I've always wanted to touch you", and she did so, with a level of intensity I hadn't known before. Her carnal pleasures were all encompassing, and the ways that she pleased me, were an inspiration, especially as she said from a POV position with my tool in her hand "mmm it's like a big ole candy bar" which she proceeded to devour. I was motivated to give of myself, and we excited each other's bodies until the next day dawned.

The time we had left in the Dell's no longer revolved around the day's planned activities. Instead, our minds were focused on when we could launch into outer space again!! We were fully and completely hooked. The only thing left was to figure out our next step. What would happen when we got home?

I've never really been one to regret my actions, but goddamn, I need to leave well enough alone sometimes! I've long since realized sometimes a fling is just that! At the time I was unaware of the concept so we flirted, and looked into each other's eyes all the way home. There was some light banter on the ride to Chicago. During our conversation, Candi mentioned that she was looking for a place to stay. Right away my sister said, "You can stay with me." Candi agreed. Given that my sister lived downstairs from me, life – I thought – would get interesting.

For some reason, we decided to keep our affair a secret. Night after night we had our secret rendezvous, enjoying the closest thing to the euphoria that either of us had experienced. Life was awesome! There were cooked meals and high spirits. We had a little commune of sorts. My sister and her man, with his daughter, Candi with her two kids, and me with my son, all living in the building. We worked together to make each other's lives easier. For a while, it worked.

There were peaks and valleys, but my love – or better yet, my trust – for Candi was solid. I didn't see anything stopping a natural progression of our relationship. The next phase, however, would be the beginning of the end; moreover, a life lesson that would change everything about my world forever... again.

For a time, Candi and I had both been looking work. She scored first, getting a job as the head of security in a downtown office building. As a man, I naturally felt some kind of way about that. But, I was quickly comforted by Candi's telling me that "taking care of the kids *was* a job!" I was Mr. Fucking Mom!!

Honestly, I enjoyed every minute. I helped the kids with their homework, cooked most of the meals, and kept the house clean – at least I tried. I especially looked forward to making Candi feel special when she got home. I hooked her up with a hot bath and delicious meals, just like I *knew* she would have done for me.

The first domino fell when I began to notice – after weeks of ironing her uniform and polishing her shoes – that my *lady* looked like a dude E-V-E-R-Y D-A-Y. She wore slacks with a button down shirt, necktie, and blazer. That was her uniform. I started to lose interest. Whether consciously, or unconsciously, I created a space between us in the bedroom. In addition, I had developed a horrible sinus infection. The effects of my illness made me super self-conscious about my breath; and consequently, the deep, passionate, dizzying kisses faded into memories. Candi and I weren't the same anymore.

I spoke with Candi about my sinus related, bad-breath complex, and she rushed to comfort me. "Sweetheart, I've never smelled your breath" she said, "its okay." I was reassured, and a little more at ease.

Still, we were not as Kissy-Kissy as before. Candi understood.

Life went on, and although the uniform completely blew me, she was my lady and I loved her. In retrospect, I know now that I missed an opportunity – BIG TIME. As her man, if *my* woman was dressed in a way that wasn't appealing to me, I should have offered a solution, rather than internalizing and creating distance. Perhaps I should have bought her a dress, or some shoes, SOMETHING! As cliché as it sounds, *you live and learn* – that is, if you're lucky!

Days, weeks, and months passed on. Candi was pulling double shifts. Her boss was calling the house so often, that I became protective. Seriously, the woman had to sleep sometime. "Don't you have someone else to cover that shift," I would ask. Despite my frustration, the calls persisted. Candi worked ALL the time. The second domino was falling fast.

I spent most of my days raising the kids. It was hard, but we had a lot of fun. The time with her kids, and especially my own son, was incredibly fulfilling.

By this time, sex was little more than an afterthought. Week after week flew by, with me tending to the kids, and Candi working – *always working*. It was all a blur.

More dominos tumbled over when I got sick, very sick. Candi left my side to go and pick up her check from work, and said she would go to Walgreens for to get me some medicine. Two hours passed. I called, but she wasn't picking up the phone 4 more hours passed, still nothing!. When she finally got home, I went nuts! I yelled, "How could you leave me like this all day and not even call?!!" We got into a knockdown, drag out fight. Nobody got hurt, physically, but shit got said, and Candi decided that it was best that she stay with her mom. I had ATTITUDE, "Get out then!" I shouted.

In my solitude, I realized that I missed Candi. I missed the kids. I missed *my* family. So we got back together. Things were cool, but still she worked a lot. During all of this, I began working at a semi- upscale furniture store on the Mag Mile just a few blocks from where Candi worked. However reconciliation was NOT helped by this Sgt. So-and-So who called the house too frequently for my taste. We argued more and more. She left with the kids every other week, and soon announced that she was leaving for good. Naturally, I was upset. I still wanted to reconcile, but when she came to pick up her things she came with Sgt. What's His Face. It suddenly became clear; the long hours, the frequent phone calls. The other man was at my doorstep. I knew, at that moment, that I had made this easy for him. Candi was a "GOOD" woman, and with her telling *war* stories, all Sgt. Jerk Face had to do was the opposite of everything I had been doing. DAMN!! My bullshit became his blueprint.

I went through a thing – full out binge drinking, crying, and bothering my people at all hours of the night. If I could have physically crawled under a rock, I literally would have. Work was hard too. Sometimes I'd get so overcome; I'd just go back home. It was too much. I could see her building from the windows of my job.

Occasionally, Candi would call me. I called her too, and even stopped by a few times. She would tell me that she missed me, and that she wanted to come 'home'. But we knew better. In conversation Candi stated that she knew that if she came back, there would be "mayhem." Candi told too many lies to justify her leaving. She'd lied to her brother, her mother, her sister, and her friends. She told so many lies, that if she had come back, everyone would have thought she was INSANE. I understood. The situation had gotten bigger than it should have. I took slight comfort in the fact that she had been honest with me, and left it alone.

A week later, while I was at work, I noticed a man walk around. He appeared to be browsing. Being the consummate professional, I welcomed him, but didn't impose. Eventually, the guy asked for my help. I went straight into sales mode, telling him about the best sofa, and explaining the differences between cherry and mahogany. He seemed preoccupied, then finally looked at me and said, "You know, sometimes a man's got to see his woman with another man before he knows it's over!" "Pardon me!?" I said, but I had heard him loud and clear. He didn't repeat himself. Instead, he promptly thanked me for my time and left. I never knew if Sgt. Asshole sent him, or

Candi, or both of them; but at that point, someone was having fun fucking with me for some reason.

I had stopped not calling, and there were no more unannounced visits, so why must you twist the proverbial knife. Whatever the cause, they had won. Although I didn't understand that shit, I never pursued the matter. I knew that, as a couple, we'd made our mistakes, had our differences, and consequently grown apart. But, I also knew that I hadn't done anything to warrant what I considered to be next level cruelty.

Time passed, and I began to resurface. I also began to redefine myself as a man. Since I worked on Michigan Avenue, I decided to teach myself about the finer things in life – taking a note from my mentors. I was excited to be getting out of my comfort zone took and into some really cool places. I dined, alone, at the top restaurants, reading while I was waiting for my dinner. I shopped for expensive clothes and began to furnish my home with "lifestyle" pieces. I felt good. I felt renewed. And, I was prepared. But for what?!

Back at work one day, a familiar, and all too painful, scenario was repeated. I was completely blindsided, and totally unaware of what was coming. Just like before, as I was at sitting my desk, a customer walked by. As usual, I acknowledged her presence and offered my assistance. After she circled the floor, she returned to my desk and smiled. She was an Asian woman – late 40's early 50's – with a kind face. She looked at me and said, "So, you're seeking a different path, huh?" I'm sure she wanted to laugh at my expression, because I was indeed seeking enlightenment, in my effort to come out of my emotional tailspin I read everything from Ilyanla Van Zant to Chopra; and admittedly had found comfort. That's why her statement struck me like those pitch black broomstick shots from my mom back in the day. She handed me a business card and said that she'd be happy to help me along my journey. The card was from a Buddhist sanctuary, and my introduction to Buddhism. My understanding and perspective began to change. "Finally," I thought, "someone positive, someone who could *see* me!" I still practice Buddhism to this day, that's how I learned that enlightenment would help me get a lot of this sand out of of my glass!

I continued to enrich my mind, body, and spirit. I was feeling somewhat vindicated and relaxed. Then, one afternoon, while I was at home sitting on the back porch, my sister said a name I still did not want to hear. "How would you feel if Candi was in jail?" she asked. I uttered an uninspired, "I'd be sorry to hear that," and that was all I had to say. But she went on talking. She told me that, after moving in with Sgt. Fuck Face and his five kids, there was trouble in 'paradise'. Evidently, one of his children didn't care for the new living arrangements. The kid hated it so much that she called the police and told them that Candi was physically abusing them. Subsequently, Child Protective Services took the kids while they investigated the allegations. Candi *and* Sgt. Dumbass were in the slammer.

Hearing the news, I realized that spitefulness was no longer in me like it was as a child; which was supported by the Buddhist teachings I had absorbed. My duty was to be the best person I could be, and let the universal Karma handle the rest. They're fine now, thankfully. They eventually married and, are presumably living the dream.

Without the pain of my experience with Candi, I would not be who I am today. Certainly, through my encounter, I reached a deeper level of understanding, one that led to some interesting, yet spiritually nourishing moments. I felt as if life was scooping some of the sand out of my water.

In my continued effort to beautify my home, and bring life into it, I decided to buy a dozen African Violets. On the way home from work one day, while walking down Michigan Avenue, several ladies saw the flowers, smiled and said, "*She's* a lucky lady." Of course, there was no *she*. But, I smiled politely anyhow. After the fourth lady stopped to acknowledge the violets, I said to her, "Please accept this from me, and have a wonderful evening."

By the time I got to my train – about a mile away – I had given away all of the flowers. I felt at peace, and realized that my actions might just have had a positive effect on people's lives. I hoped that, perhaps they would pass that positivity on to others. It just felt good. I still give of myself – patience, understanding, and love – because just like those flowers, there are people who need them, so I give unselfishly and selfishly enrich my soul, that's the yin and yang if you will. And ME – I'm cool with the path I must walk!

I Wish I May…,

I had spent the better part of two years getting my shit together, and I had since become a product of my environment. The trouble was that I had two very different environments; one, the increasingly deprived 'hood', and the other the affluent, upscale, Michigan Avenue. I likened my daily commute to traveling in Europe, from France to Germany – different languages, different cultures, even different food. This was my life, day after day. But, I was comfortable in both places. In those days, I was feeling better than ever! I had quit smoking, started exercising, and gained 15 pounds – mostly muscle. All my troubles were disappearing in life's rear view mirror.

I wasn't making big money, but I was doing alright. Like most people, I looked forward to tax time – new clothes, new shoes –PARTY TIME! I went to a local tax preparer who, for some reason, directed me to their Hyde Park office. At the desk was one of the prettiest women I'd ever seen. I had an instant crush; sweaty palms, nervousness, dry mouth - a full out, schoolboy crush!

May was a cross between Faith Evans and Mary J. Blige. She was super sexy! We went over my documents together. She was more aggressive than I however, the chemistry was definitely there. Although nothing transpired from our first encounter, Uncle Sam soon brought us together. An agent at her office had used my information to defraud the I.R.S., so she contacted me and asked that I come in to discuss the matter personally.

Before I got there, she'd ordered a pizza. It was delivered in the middle of our discussion. She opened the box, right on her desk, then looked at me and asked "Would you like a slice?" "HELL YEAH," I thought to myself, "and I'd like some pizza too." We talked for hours – business and personal – and exchanged numbers. May was too fine. I couldn't wait to call, but I was skeptical. *If* social media had been around, her status would've been listed as *complicated*. During our chat, May described herself as being "available, but involved". I wasn't comfortable. I wrestled with the notion of calling her. And, when she called me, I didn't answer. That was that, but I couldn't stop thinking about her. There is no grey area for me in regard to your status you either committed or not. Given what I had gone through with Candi I had vowed NEVER to be a guy like Sgt. Dickhead

About two months later, I gave in and dialed her number. May was happy to hear from me, but she wondered aloud why I hadn't called sooner. I explained myself and she promptly informed me that she had severed her ties and was officially uninvolved. *UNINVOLVED!* COOL!!

We met at my place for cocktails and conversation. When she sat down, I helped her take off her shoes, and put a pillow underneath her feet – a move I'd picked up in Mexico. She LOVED it! After a few hours, she had to leave. As I escorted her to the front door, she reached back and felt me, whispering, "I want you". The feeling was mutual alright, but we were out of time.

Our next encounter was hot and heavy. May was so pretty, and very accommodating. At the time, I didn't have a bed frame, so my bed on the floor – don't ask. We lay down, kissed, and made love for hours. When May reached her peak, her juices flowed into my mouth like the waters of the Mississippi River. My sheets were drenched with love's liqueur. We were covered in sweat. Her body glistened, as the moonlight crept through my bedroom window. I was falling; I was head over heels. Still, I knew I had to teach myself a new trick. I had to perfect bringing her to orgasm *without* drinking her nectar. Because, who does *that*?

A couple of days later, in the middle of the night, the phone rang. It was May. She had been arrested for a D.U.I and needed my help (here's one of those traffic signals; I believe the color would be yellow). She asked if I could pick her up. I hurried out the door to her rescue! We went back to my place and initiated another round of hot-blooded, steamy lovemaking. We went at it all night long.

When we woke up, I was pleased to find May at my *service*. Her performance was mediocre, comparatively; not bad, but far from great. This became her morning ritual. Once, after her a.m. antics were complete, she asked me, "What kind of guy doesn't want head when they wake up?" She was referring to her past relationship, but obviously noticing a lack of enthusiasm on my part. So, I responded, "the kind of guy who's not getting top-shelf head!" And, thus began May's training. She wanted to learn; she wanted to be the *best*. And, I wanted to teach her. I told her that, after perfecting certain techniques, to add her own style and finesse. "When you're at your best, no man should be able to withstand your talents for more than five minutes… the amount of time you spend should *always* be up to you!" I explained. May was a fast learner, and practice truly made perfect. If I had had the proper accreditation, she would've graduated Magna *cum* Laude. Things progressed and we became an item. But, what I failed to mention is that in the meantime, I had met Cheryl (oddly enough, a security guard) at work.

Cheryl and May were opposites in every way. She was an attractive, country-thick woman who wore little make-up, if any at all. She was passive and very soft spoken. Cheryl was an undiscovered talent –

that's what I call the women who don't flaunt their physical attributes. *Ladies* like her would never even consider wearing a dress with low cleavage, or a skirt that was too short. They hide behind jogging pants and over-sized sweaters. But when they take off their clothes, GOOD GOOGLY WOOGLEY!!! Cheryl was no exception. When she took off her top for the first time, her breasts were looked up to greet the sunshine! I liked her a lot.

Her legs were thick and muscular, but soft as silk; and, she was a Capricorn. *My extensive, non-scientific, investigations have shown me that Capricorns will do WHATEVER they have to in order to please you.* One evening, I went to meet Cheryl for a late night rendezvous. Knowing her willingness to please, I had prepared a goodie-bag, of sorts. In it, was a pair of leather pumps and a trench coat. When she got in the car she gave me a soft kiss and a warm hug – that woman put her arms around me like no one else. When we got close to my house, I looked at her and asked, "Are you ready?" "For what," she replied. I studied her face as I handed her the bag and said, "To be ravaged."

She took off her clothes in the car while I drove through the alley to the back of my house. I eased her thick toes into the yellow heels, I'd gotten for her. Then, she slid into the trench coat. I pulled around to the corner and said, "Get out of the car!" She was dumbfounded. I explained that I LOVED to watch her walk, and that her legs were, like sculpted mahogany. "I wanna watch you walk to my house," I told her. She smiled, and got to stepping', as I cruised behind her. The block was teeming with people that night, and Cheryl was just as excited by our pseudo-voyeuristic game, as I was.

When we got upstairs, I grabbed her by the hand and led her outside to the back porch where I ripped her trench coat open, revealing her voluptuous frame. I pulled her face to mine and gave her a kiss that seemed to last an eternity. I pulled her head back by her ponytail, exposing her neck, licked her gently from the collarbone to the earlobe, then whispered, "Turn around." I knelt down and devoured her from behind. Her heavy, caramel colored breasts danced over the banister. There is a main thoroughfare across from the vacant lot behind my house, so anyone driving or walking by could have seen her.

Cheryl was such a tasty treat. She would always beg for me to stop, while at the same time, reaching behind to grab my head and keep me there. When she was ready, I stood with one hand forcefully pulling her ponytail back and the other fondling the petals of her flower while I pounded her from behind. Her legs buckled. The explosive orgasms left us trembling. We were both spent. Cheryl was my favorite; we shared the same mentality. Our escapades were a blissful balance of sadomasochistic sensuality; she loved to bite, and I loved how she would jam her meaty toes into my mouth when she stroked me until I popped .

Meanwhile, May's aggressive nature simply was unrivaled. She *demanded* that we see each other. And, before I knew it, we were "together".

Compared to mine, May's family was large. That meant I often had to be social. Yuck! Her family embraced me right away, and I loved them too. May's mom was especially sweet; she was that *cool* mom. Every neighborhood has one. I LOVE THAT WOMAN!

Early in our relationship, May invited me over to a family gathering. It was all love, when I arrived, good music, good food, and PLENTY of shit talking. I was HOME! There were a lot of people there and, since I didn't really know anybody, I decided to chill and observe. After a while, I saw a dude moving through the crowd. He was visibly upset. I watched him work his way through the crowd, and remember thinking, "Damn, he's gonna fuck somebody up!" I watched him get closer, and realized, this motherfucker was coming for me! I stood to meet him, but May's brother grabbed him pulled out his gun. He told the dude, it was time for him to leave. "Who was HE," I wondered. He was the infamous BABY DADDY!! I should've known, but I *can* be a little naïve at times. It turned out that the break-up wasn't something HE was comfortable with or even real- I had been tricked. Whatever though; I loved me some May.

As our relationship grew, I doted over May. There was nothing I wouldn't do for her; we were deeply in love. Unfortunately, though, I lost my downtown job. I was unemployed for nearly a year. I eventually was given the opportunity to teach art to children in grades kindergarten through eighth. Although I had never taught before, my mom was an accomplished educator and beloved administrator for decades. I learned a lot from her.

I was back in business. My first paycheck, $15,000, was for the entire semester! I was RICH! – That day. I went to get May for an impromptu shopping spree! When we got to the mall, I took great pride in saying "Get whatever you want baby!" I wasn't expecting what happened next. She spent all of $600.00 – that was it. I encouraged her to do more, but she was "good". May's restraint broadened my perspective, and opened my heart to her in a new way. She wasn't greedy. On the way home, she thanked me for everything, and said, "Baby I have you, and that's all I'll ever need!"

PERFECT!!

May had made it clear that she loved me. So, on the night that I called and got no response – highly unusual – I worried. Out of concern, I committed the cardinal sin – I went to her place unannounced. I know, I know. But at the time, it seemed perfectly logical. I drove up and noticed her car parked out front, and the lights on in her bedroom. I could see someone moving around, but May still did not answer her phone! I rang the bell. Surely my new family, who had embraced me so fully, would let me in right? Nope, I was told that she wasn't home. Her brother *escorted* me out, where we had a long talk. The situation became clear. May was cheating!

What was I supposed to do? For years I had proven myself. I studied Buddhism which taught me to understand that people are just being themselves based on their own state of evolution, so I could not place fault, nor relate said evolution to mine, I had fallen in love! I had no choice, so I swallowed it. After all, there *was* Cheryl, so my efforts to avoid a nomination for the Hypocrite of the Year Award led me to complete fairness, to myself at least, I should have thought about Cheryl. However, May and I were *even*.

I decided that unconditional love was what I wanted, so I knew I had to give it. I believed that marriage vows took effect long before the ceremony. For better or worse and all the rest, I was all in. What

May didn't know was that, with regard to her sexual ideology, we were equals. Like me, she wasn't trying to start side relationships, she just liked to fuck! And I caught her, time and time again.

Among the things we discussed was the fact that I have a sixth sense about people. When I care someone, I get a 'vibe' if something is out of the ordinary. It sounds crazy, I know, but she'll tell you, I have NEVER been wrong. With that in mind, I posed the question "Why are you so sloppy?" She never offered an excuse. Everybody knew what she was doing, but I stood with my head up because my baby wasn't malicious. She was just being herself. Her most infamous saying was "I'm not girlfriend material." But, I was NOT trying to hear that. I believed that if I wanted to selfishly hold on to love, I had to *unselfishly* give it to May. Perhaps one day she'll have some to give me in return. *At least that was my hope.*

I went all out to show my love for May. Once, I spent hours cutting out paper hearts, each with a different reason for loving her. I laid them on the stairs, creating a path from the bottom to the top.

Then, atop the staircase, she was met with a bouquet of balloons, filled with trinkets – including a ring. We stayed together, for a while. We loved. We fought. There was a constant back and forth of good times and bad.

One Valentine's Day, I decided to drop off flowers to May's office. When I walked in, the other ladies in the office looked at me as if I was crazy. But, their gawking soon turned into green-eyed, covetous glares. I got to May's desk and I saw that she already had flowers. When I asked her where, or *whom*, they had come from she sharply replied, "Mike, this guy I used to see." The truth was she still saw Mike from time to time, and everybody in the office knew it. We argued, and I told her that I would *never* bring her flowers on Valentine's Day again – EVER! That's right. I didn't end the relationship. I didn't say, "It's over, fuck you!" Her punishment was simple, *no more flowers*. Crazy!

A year passed. But, I hadn't forgotten my promise. I also hadn't forgotten what flowers meant to me. So, the next Valentine's Day I marched into that same office with balloons and flowers. May's smile was as big as the sun. She said, "Thank you for doing this for me baby," as I walked away. I turned to her and said "Baby, I didn't do this for you. I did this for me!" I worked hard to understand love and build my virtues, as a man. I could not afford to lock my love and virtues away forever, so I gave.

Throughout our relationship, I forged my own 'mini-friendships' with May's friends and family. They weren't my *real* friends, of course; their loyalty was to May. One evening, May's best friend, Kay, confided in me. She propositioned me, asking that *I* teach her how to perform a sexual act similar to what I'd taught May. An interesting opportunity had presented itself, and I had a choice – love or revenge. Naturally, I chose love.

I rejected Kay's advances, but we did talk, and that's when shit got interesting. She revealed a recent conversation, she had with May, via text, in which May professed that she had always loved *her*, wanted to be in a relationship with *her*, but just didn't know how! WOW! Kay, my 'mini-friend', who *I* had foolishly confided in, was the one MAY *always* loved? And, *she* loved May. What Tha Fuck?!

I confronted May with this newly divulged information, and copped to everything about my conversation with Kay. I threw her friend right under the bus, and even disclosed the side deal her "*love*" tried to cut. FUCK HER!! When the smoke cleared, we stood there together. There was definitely still love between us.

Things cooled down, and over time, we developed a greater understanding of each other. When I say *we*, I mean ME. I knew May was still up to her old, sloppy tricks, and I was a bit standoffish; especially as it related to unannounced visits. But May had an interesting perspective. She said, "We've been together almost ten years. You don't have to call me baby, just come when you want."

I fought the urge for a long time. One night, though, after partying at the club, I decided I wanted to see my baby. So, I went to her house. I called, but there was no answer. When I knocked, her daughter opened the door and invited me in. I knocked on her bedroom door and – no response. I sat for a while and even twisted the knob a little. May was a sound sleeper, especially when she'd been drinking, so I sat a while longer.

Her mom walked by and I asked, "What should I do Ma?" She shrugged her shoulders. I knocked one more time. Finally, the door opened, and standing in front of May was a dude wielding a knife! Before I knew it, he stabbed me twice! Fortunately, I had my .25 in my back pocket. I took two steps back, cocked, and aimed at his right eye – he froze. I heard her mother speak to me, "Baby, you don't want to do that," she said. Then, the same three kids I'd known for *ten years* rose up against me with force. May's mom spoke again, "Just leave baby, he called the police." So, I left.

I exited the house as the police pulled up. It had been raining, so there were big, deep puddles outside of May's house. I dropped my piece (. 25) into a puddle just as the officers approached me. "They said you had a gun sir. Is that right?" the officer said. I presented my sliced up jacket and showed him my wounds. "If I had a gun, don't you think I would've shot him?" I asked. Then I told him I wanted to press charges, even though I no intentions of doing so.

And that was it. In three minutes – 180 seconds – my ten year relationship with May came to a head. It was over, or so I thought. Eight months later, I received a text from May stating how much she appreciated my constant, unconditional love. I typed, "I will love you forever, I would do it all again." But would I? I later came to find out that the guy in May's room insisted on pressing charges... at least that's what the officer who requested fellatio from May told her, in order for the paperwork to get lost... and she granted his request. There unbeknownst to me; was an unfortunate display the love and loyalty I had always wished for.

One More Chance

Reeling from the break up with May, I found myself not wanting to be with anyone. It seems that I always take a break between relationships. This time, though, I didn't become a recluse or crawl under that proverbial rock. I went out a lot, but I didn't allow myself to get too involved with anyone; nor did I allow anyone to get too attached to me.

I wondered if I was a manifestation of my born day, April 1st. Was I just an April FOOL? Why had I stood with May for so long? Not to be misleading, after about the third time a caught May in the midst of her carelessly concealed transgressions, I did my share of dirt; continuing, for example, to nurture my on-again, off-again relationship with Cheryl. I was feeling gun shy, and in my apprehension, I declared that no woman would have the opportunity to meet *'the little boy'* – a nickname for my love, because he wants and deserves the things I never had: acceptance, understanding, care and protection.

I also felt the need to create an alter ego. Thus, *Chance* was born. *He* was result of everything I had learned from my esteemed mentors, plus the knowledge gained through my life experiences. Understanding how to cultivate joy and tolerate pain, how to please others, and how to leave a woman feeling good about *her*, Chance was a machine, who didn't give a fuck. His Mantra, "I am what you see!" conveyed confidence. Chance was self-assured, well-groomed and impeccably dressed. *He* could charm the pants off any woman in three minutes flat. I unleashed *Chance* two, sometimes three, nights a week. Women were enamored by his swagger, and guys dubbed him the "Boss" player. He was. Most nights, he had an entourage of women, all with whom he danced and flirted with fervently. There were one stands and menage a trois every weekend. Why not? Who gave a shit about what *Chance* was doing? NOBODY! As a matter of fact, *his* exploits were regarded as top level shit! But there was one condition. Anything done must be deeply rooted in the truth. I, *Chance*, was always truthful.

One night, while out with four women – all with whom I had been intimate – a fifth woman, sitting across the bar, was flirting. She motioned for me to come over – enter *Chance*. When I approached her, she asked, "Are you here alone?" "I'm here with them," I said, pointing to my circle of four. She gave me her number, and said, "Maybe you should call me when you're ready to be exclusive," Interesting, I thought. I told her that the women I was with enjoyed me the way I am, and that they were with me because of the way I make them feel – physically and emotionally. And I asked her, "Why would I give them up for something *exclusive*? Would you?" I continued "Imagine if you had a guy who stimulated your intellect, another guy who romanced you, and another guy who satisfied you would you give them all up on the off chance that I might be the one for you?" I paused and said "If *YOU* would like to join *US*, they will welcome you just as I will, and if not I'm certainly flattered by the attention you have given me!" and with that I smiled, got the bartender's eye...and told him that her next round was on me." Chance's confident strength, mixed with his honesty and crystal-clear, point-blank style of communication, became his calling card. He wanted women, and he got them. His *'love me or leave me'* persona empowered the women to make their choice. If a woman chose to leave however, it would never be because he was caught with someone else, or because they were misled. Quite the contrary, it was what it was – open and honest, cut and dry. Or so he thought.

Keep It On The Table

On an evening when one of my guys needed a wingman, I hung out with him at a nearby lounge. It was cool. I did a lot of flirting, and had a good time. Sitting next to me was a light skinned sister with twists in her hair. Her name was Linda, she was very pretty – silky, soft skin and just the right amount of cleavage. Linda wasn't a prissy girl. She was very attractive, with a real "earth" vibe; she looked like she was into poetry and incense. We chatted for a while, standard nightclub talk, and I really didn't think it was going to go anywhere. I got up to go to the restroom, and she asked if I was leaving. I told her that I was going to 'powder my nose'. She laughed and said she'd hold my seat. I took that as a sign of interest, but found out that she was just trying to get a seat for one of her girls!

When I returned, I shifted my energy to the girl sitting two seats down from Linda – who, by the way, strangely enough could've been Trisha's long lost sister! I watched as she found ingenious ways to make eye contact with me, despite the fact that there was a guy blatantly vying for her attention. Knowing that she wouldn't be able to talk, I gave her the *'write your number down'* signal. She saw me and smiled. I asked Linda to watch my seat and, as I walked past her, she discreetly handed me the *digits*. I circled the bar and returned to my seat, right next to Linda.

This time our conversation was a lot more engaging. I started off, "Did you see that shit!?" She laughed and said, "Well, I guess y'all got something in common!" I knew what she meant, but I let her get her dig in! "And what's that,' I asked her. "It means both y'all ain't shit!!" she said laughing. She wasn't being judgmental, this lady was different. As our conversation continued I told her, "You have until I get down to here on my drink to ask me questions, because after that I'm liable to say anything!" She thought that was funny. We continued to feel each other out. There was definitely something different about her, but I couldn't put my finger on it.

A couple of days later, I texted her a message – "Call me." She did. We had great conversations. Linda was a very attentive listener and easy to talk to, qualities that would prove valuable later. She got me to open up about May and all that transpired in that relationship. She was reassuring, and emotionally supportive, while still letting me feel like a grown man. She was amazing.

Linda was in the midst of ending her current relationship as we established an alliance of our own. Neither of us wanted a relationship, but we both enjoyed each other's company and appreciated having a genuine sense of companionship.

We hit the streets together with one guiding principle, "Keep *everything* on the table." For some people, that could mean that some issues were discussed and others were off limits, but our friendship was different. Everything really meant *EVERYTHING*. We liked going out together; we liked hanging out. People often thought we were a couple, and in a sense – I suppose – we were. We slept together frequently, and really understood each other as people. Not wanting "exclusivity," we kept things open and honest. That proved to be more difficult than we expected, for both of us.

Our escapades began one night when we were out together, kickin' it, at a local spot. I ran into one of my guys, scoping out this tall good looking girl. As much as I would like to tell you what that our conversation entailed, I cannot. I was blasted! All I know is that the four of us ended up at my place somehow. I remember that, by the time I took off my jacket, Linda and my guy were already going' to work on this chick! I joined in and indulged myself in our new friend, as they fell back. Out of the corner of my eye, I noticed Linda pleasuring my friend. Everybody was having a great time and, when it was done, we all went our separate ways.

A few days later, while I was shooting' the shit at another friend's house – we affectionately call it the dungeon – Linda called and asked what I was up to. "Just chillin', I responded. She asked if she and a friend could come through and, of course, I said yes. My friend and I had met two ladies the night before while we're out, and coincidentally, one of them called and asking if she too could swing by. Linda and her friend were already there, so I took a pause, put her on hold and asked Linda if she wouldn't mind me having more guests. "Of course not baby," she replied, "Do you!" I got back on the phone I informed her she was more than welcome to come by. I told her that I was entertaining at the moment, that there were women at my place who were interested in me, and in whom I was interested. It didn't take any convincing. I spoke the truth! With that, she was on her way!

About 30 minutes later, the *other* girl we'd met the night before, phoned and asked if SHE could stop over! Everybody was cool with it! So there I was, with three women; all with whom I'd been intimate. There were no hiding; no lies. There was no stress, just good conversation and good times. YES!

Linda was more than passing fancy. She was always there when the smoke cleared. She had always had my back, despite my resistance! We talked all day, every day, for the good part of 6 months. But, now and then, I felt the need to say to her, "You know you're not my girlfriend right?" That was because Linda did a lot of 'girlfriend stuff', from taking *me* out with her friends *and* mine for karaoke on my birthday, to making sure I had eaten. She'd re-introduced me to the wonderful world of homemaking, showed me how to organize my crib. Hell, she even fixed my credit! She did these things, all while being the most patient and understanding friend, I could imagine. But she was NOT my girlfriend.

Our sexual encounters grew to be other-worldly. For a time, she too required some coaching. But, to her credit, she was an exceptional student. The energy between us was fantastic. Our sessions were intense, and went on for hours. They often involved mild choking, submission, and just plain nastiness.

However, we chose to indulge, we were always left dripping in sweat!

Finally, the acceptance, understanding, care, and protection that I longed for had arrived. I was giving it, unconditionally, and it was being reciprocated! Our friendship was symbiotic. Things got interesting as our relationship flourished. Friends and loved ones noticed our bond, and soon began to question or the nature of our union.

The very people who questioned our relationship, and 'looked upside our heads,' were either unhappy or dissatisfied with their own. It was hard for them to wrap their psyches around an honest, open relationship. They couldn't conceive of it! My friends pulled me aside, saying, "You see what she's doing right?!" And, her friends were no different. They would grab her and ask "Girl, you ain't gon' say NOTHIN'?!" We thought they were hilarious! On the rare occasion that we would try and explain our connection, people crunched up their faces in confusion as if *we* had somehow gone mad. The reality is, we thought *they* were the nut-balls. We had a clear, birds-eye view of their bullshit. TEN out of TEN times, they were either being deceptive or being deceived. So, the fact that *they* had the unmitigated gall to have footnotes and sidebars for *us* always made for a good laugh!

Keeping everything on the table felt right! It worked for us. We didn't have to sneak around. There was no accounting for lost time, or tracking people down. Instead, there was transparency. We'd call each other and announce, "I'm about to have company. I call you when I'm done!" Sometimes, we'd lay the phone down and eavesdrop on each other's trysts. We were freaky, and thoroughly enjoyed every minute.

Our relationship was thriving, and soon encompassed other aspects of my life, including my business and my health. Linda wouldn't allow me to be on any bullshit when it came to either. She took the reins, and I followed her lead. "Oh, you wanna patent your invention?" she asked, "Here, I filled out the paperwork. Read it, sign it, and give it back to me!" Done! "You need to go to the doctor," she observed, "The appointment's already been made, I took the day off, and I'll pick you up at 11am." DONE! And when that appointment led to my having surgery, it was Linda, who took me to the hospital. She waited during the operation, and she was there when I opened my eyes. She even took me for a cheeseburger and a chocolate shake on the way home. This woman was beyond belief!

One evening, Linda was supposed to meet me at our neighborhood lounge for drinks. She called to let me know that she was at another party, and was running late. It was no problem. I could easily hold down the fort. Another hour later, Linda called again. She was pulling up, but parking was at a minimum. She asked me to come out and hold a spot for her and ensure her safety the neighborhood was a tad unsavory. I stepped out, lit a cigarette, and watched dutifully as she opened her door. Then, the passenger door opened.

Linda brought a friend along – a thick, 6 foot tall woman, with creamy, Hershey brown skin. Her short black dress accentuated her powerful legs. I watched the taut muscles of her legs flex as she walked toward me. This girl was sexy!

I opened the door for the ladies and Linda looked at me with a cunning grin. As she walked by, I asked, "Who's this?!" Without breaking her stride she turned back and said "THAT's for you!" REMARKABLE! Linda was absolutely awesome.

Love without condition, the investments I made finally turned a profit! Finally, somebody accepted me, good, bad, and in-between. I pulled Linda to the side and took a moment to express *my* appreciation, telling Linda that she had single-handedly changed my heart – and my life.

The night ended with an after party at my place. We sat down on the couch together, and with little hesitation Linda initiated the proceedings. She started with the slow motion as my Amazonian gift kissed me like we were on our honeymoon. Linda arose, offering me to our guest, who happily obliged. The kiss I had so thoroughly enjoyed was upgraded to oral euphoria. In a dreamlike state, I closed my eyes and watched the fireworks explode. Linda held her hair and watched Amazonia's chocolate silk derrière glimmer in the moonlight. It was a beautiful night.

Generally, Linda was perceived as the innocent victim of *Chance's* exploits. But, truthfully, she had her fair share of fun. Quiet as kept, Linda was a fully invested participant, who had an entourage of her own. And, while I frequently teased her about her veil of 'purity,' what started as jokes, soon became a rift. Even in a polyamorous relationship, jealousy can rear its ugly head.

I came to resent the fact that Linda could immerse herself in "our" naughty little world and conveniently, return to Linda-land squeaky clean. And what's worse, I was slowly finding out that maybe *everything* wasn't on the table. We had a spat, but quickly moved passed it and life continued.

Anna One, Anna Two…

One rainy night, after club hopping, I decided to make a final stop – my good ol' neighborhood lounge. I was out alone and, as I walked towards the spot, I noticed a curvaceous figure walking my way. She was shielding her hair from the rain and carefully sidestepping the cracks in the walkway in her stylish platform heels. It was Anna. Our paths crossed and our eyes met. With my gaze locked on her, I removed my blazer. She smiled as I covered her hair, a said "I got you babe." I escorted her to her car. She got in and rolled down the window, then looked up at me. The darkness and the rain seemed to disappear.

I looked at her, beneath the orange glow of street lights, and saw the most entrancing honey colored eyes I'd ever seen. We exchanged some idle chatter. She said that she hadn't really had a good time that night, but, "Look what a treasure I've found." I was flattered. I asked her if she was done for the night, and invited her to my after-hours spot, the dungeon. She was all for it, so we chilled there for a while.

One thing I know is that the dungeon is NO *dungeon.* It's very nice! My friend and I painstakingly thought out the décor. In our man-cave I'd painted a giant Scarface mural at the entrance, there were black leather sofas, flat-screen televisions, custom floors, and a fully stocked bar. In the back was the Red Room, used for private sessions. We left no stone unturned.

When women walked into the dungeon, they were impressed by their surroundings. Anna enjoyed the ambience. We sat down, had a couple of drinks, and talked for a while. Our attraction could not be denied, so we left the dungeon headed to my place.

My home was a clear reflection of my life's influences. The Zen-inspired furniture, wall fountains, and tastefully crafted leather walls in the bedroom of my apartment was my way of paying homage to my mentors – the elegance of Uncle Lucky, the simplicity of my father, and the artistic touch of Mr. Drake. My home was my tribute. When people enter my apartment, they feel calm and relaxed. A nod of affirmation from my Uncle Lucky during a visit was a proud moment for me.

Anna and I sipped on another cocktail and shared a little more conversation. I was drawn to her. She had a warm, welcoming way about her, and didn't flinch at any of the bullshit I dished out. Things started to sizzle after a while, so I stood up and extended my hand and asked her to stay with me. She agreed. We stood, looking silently into each other's eyes. I had a thought and wicked smirk adorned my face. "What?" She giggled. So, my true Aries fashion, I said, "I was thinking that maybe I wanna give you some head." She stepped closer to me and said. "Hmm, maybe I wanna give YOU some head!"

I found her tenacity both provocative and amusing. We quenched each other's thirsts. Anna was gifted, to say the least. She was a woman, possessed. She wrapped her tongue around me and her eyes disappeared into her head, as if she'd entered a *fellatial the heights of pleasure trance*! I felt an exhilarating rush, and as we danced our bedroom tango, our bodies intertwined to sharing a space in the soft light of dawn. The depths of our intimacy brought on a new level of consciousness. I understood what tantric sex was all about; as did she, we sat there facing each other feeling each other's spirits as we reached the pinnacles of pleasure without touching, and I luxuriated it!

My next move was to call Linda. I wanted to tell her about my latest adventure and, of course, introduce them. Besides, she had recently expressed an interest in a banker, she'd met, and so what's fair *is* fair. We were being open and honest. EVERYTHING was on the table.

Things went well, in the sense that we all partied together *and* slept together. On a blissful morning after, I got up to prepare breakfast for everyone. While I was cooking, the ladies engaged in girl talk. I stayed out of it, thinking that if they wanted my opinion, they'd give it to me. After breakfast, the ladies posed a question. "Do you think you would be satisfied with just me and Linda?" Anna asked. With only three, maybe four, seconds to give the response – *correctly* – I said, "YES! Each of you speaks to a different part of me. With you, two, I wouldn't need anything else." I was being honest. Anna and I had a metaphysical connection, children of the sun – incense, candles, fountains, meditation – that was us. Linda was the blueprint! Her generosity and selflessness, paired with her nurturing, kind-hearted spirit, and an endless list of those *little things* that make someone truly amazing, helped redefine my perspective of women. My answer was YES, I could be TOTALLY cool with them!

We partied on. Eventually, Anna's participation began to wane. There was no specific reason, and no hard feelings. Sometimes things take off; sometimes not. We had fun fooling around and being silly together. We'd greet each other in different languages and create rhymes in our text conversations. We kept it light and fresh. It just didn't last long. Linda wondered aloud about her, asking, "What's up with Anna?" I simply replied, "Not a whole lot," and that was that.

As Linda and I moved on, there was a heavy amount of partying. Our weekends began on Thursday night and continued on until dawn on Sunday. We thoroughly enjoyed being with each other; where we were, and what we were doing, was of no consequence. Spending time with Linda never got old. We'd be together for days. With her, I always felt something I'd never felt before, serenity.

There were plenty of women for me *and* men for her. I started getting used to waking up with multiple women in my apartment. I actually ran out of robes and slippers once – Linda purchased them on my behalf – still under the not my girlfriend umbrella, however we were all relaxed and having a good time. Whether that meant a sitting and having a serious discussion, chasing each other around the house like teenagers, or having water fights, we *all* had fun.

Seeds of Resentment

I noticed that, sometimes, Linda appeared to be irritated. We started getting into spats about things seemed insignificant, and I always had to *drag* shit outta her, facts regarding her personal trysts began to become convoluted. I took offense to that because, we were friends. But, the fact that she was even fuckin with me warranted my full attention, and my compassion. So, although I felt slighted, I tried to be understanding.

One night Linda and I went to one of our usual spots to hang out. It was a good night, loads of women; I was feeling great! I saw an older woman on the other side of the bar. She had something different going on. Her head full of silver-grey hair styled to perfection, and her big, brown, Bambi eyes and a soft sexy smile screamed of sophistication. She was sitting in between her two friends, which wouldn't stop me from making a move, so I put her on my radar. I knew that I would have to tailor my approach so, as the night progressed; I kept an eye on her.

Gaining access to a woman who is surrounded by her lady-friends is high-stakes mission, *not* for the average guy. It's a major undertaking that often requires evasive maneuvers. Self-confidence, quick wit, and a thick skin are a must in these situations. Even the best of the best get shot down once in a while, and not always by the woman in pursuit. Sometimes, the girlfriends run interference.

It was time to test the waters. I passed by get a closer look. She was very attractive, but I kept it moving. I went outside for a smoke; I needed a minute to strategize. I stood there thinking, looking out to the street. Then, I pulled out a square from my chest pocket, placed between my lips, lit it, and took a puff. When I turned around, there she was – the old lady! She was so close that I nearly bumped into her. We smiled at each other. She had also stepped out for a smoke. "Allow me," I said, and I moved closer to give her a light. I complimented her on her hair and told her that I couldn't keep my eyes off her. She asked my name, and I replied, "Chance." She thought that was unique and told me her name was Stevi. We stood there mesmerized. We were lost in each other. But after a little chatter and a cigarette, it was time to head back inside. I escorted her to a seat and pulled out her chair. She sat down and, before I walked away, I told her, "If you need *anything*, just look for me and I'll fulfill your needs." Then off I went.

Later that night I walked over to follow up with Stevi. As I approached, I noticed this big dude trying to talk to her. He was not doing well – borderline obnoxious. I overheard him dishing out some stale, corny lines, so I stepped in front of him and said, "Stevi, you cool, dear?!" I turned around, looked at the dude and said" what's going on FAM! That's a bad hat you got on! (It wasn't) I motioned to the bartender. "Get my man, whatever he's having!" put it on my tab!" I gave the guy a soul shake, turned to Stevi and her friends and said "if y'all need anything... lemme know!" A sense of relief, and disbelief, washed over her face. She and her girlfriends both were impressed by the way I broke up the guy's line of bullshit. Dude was twice my size! But everyone tells me that *Chance's* swag was over six-feet tall. So, actually I *was* taller than him.

Stevi and I exchanged numbers. Within two weeks' time, we made contact. Our initial conversation was quite lengthy, and I made a point to tell her about my way of doing things. However, she was not receptive to the idea of *sharing*. I enjoyed our conversation. Stevi was intelligent and witty. And, since I've never been one to set aside, someone of value, just because they had no interest being intimate, I thanked her for her time and welcomed her to call again.

I told Linda about my conversation with Steve, and we agreed sometimes you win and sometimes you learn – losing is never an option.

A couple of days later, Stevi accepted my offer and called again. Even though, deep down, I thought she might, I was still somewhat surprised. Several conversations followed, and little by little, Stevi began to bend. "Every time we talk, you put a wrinkle in my brain," she commented. We finally agreed that it was time to meet again. I waited outside her door, and when she came out, she was gorgeous – a black skirt, sexy heels, and not a silver hair out of place! I was spellbound.

Back at my place, after a few drinks and some light conversation, I decided to give her a foot massage. I sat in front of her, and reached down to position her legs to my pillow. Right away I spotted that she didn't have on any panties. And, not only that, she had an engorged, oversized flower bud! WHAT-THA-F$&K?! As usual, I maintained my composure sort of. She would probably tell you that that was the most half-assed foot massage that she had ever received. Obviously, I was distracted! I had never seen a clit that size!

I was curious. I let my fingers do the walking, creeping slowly up her inner-thighs. She closed her eyes in quiet submission and revealed her true glory. Overcome with anticipation, I had to taste her. I kissed her softly and stroked the length of her flower with my tongue, but playtime was over. When I reached my destination, I latched on and suckled her gently, circling in hypnotic rhythm, slipping in one finger, and then another, playfully tickling her inside. Stevi sighed in agonizing pleasure. It wasn't long before she grabbed my bald head and cried out my name. She screamed.

I looked up and asked "You cool?" Stevi shot me an admonishing look, letting let me know to get back to business. I resumed the delightful deed, praising her lovely flower. She squirmed and squealed, her chest heaving with excitement; her body locked. She shuddered.

Then, in an orgasmic frenzy, Stevi leaned up and reached for my belt buckle, unfastening it with the quickness and stealth of Whodini. She was ready to show and prove, and her skills were superior — a compliment I extend with full authority. Her performance reigns supreme!

I've been *head* coach to more than a few women in my day; some were willing pupils — eager to learn, while others were inflexible know-it-alls who didn't listen to shit. Put simply, if a guy *comes* through one of your best jobs and says, casually, "That was cool," your skills are second-rate. And if, when the topic comes up in conversation, you find yourself saying, "Well, I haven't had any complaints," to you I say this, formal complaints about a head is a rarity. The average guy is just happy his Johnson sucked at all! So, that's a baseless statement. However, if your guy has attempted to slow you down so that he can enjoy your offerings and 5 minutes later, lays there motionless, with his hand across chest – thanking you - then may consider yourself highly skilled. Stevi fell into the latter category, as a matter of fact; this performance was one for the ages! Her long firm strokes as she twisted her soft hands up and down my enjoyment had me racing with excitement! As I watched her let the juices from her inviting mouth almost touch the floor before she playfully slurped them back in. I watched her, as she stole a little sweetness that dripped from her chin and skillfully used its wet warmth to fondle my jewels. Now its way too early in our session for me to tap out, so I aggressively put my hands on her cheeks, as she looked up submissively I said "bring it here!" As I helped to the bedroom, I laid her on the arm of a big chair so that her head rested on its welcoming cushion and her pleasure was completely exposed …to me! When I entered her softness she moaned at my gentle, slow, methodical stroke, and as I looked at her chocolate body; I started to explore. As my pace and force increased I reached for her plump nipples. She put her hand over mine as if to say "that's what I need! So I began to squeeze until I found her level. Since my other hand was free, I reached for her unattended girlfriend and applied the same pressure, as I twisted and pulled, she passionately dug her nails into my forearms. As the force of my strokes began to move the chair, I wrapped my hands around her ankles and held them like two handlebars. I became enticed by her pretty little candy colored toes... so I began to rhythmically suck and nibble until I could no longer resist... so I looked her in the eyes. .. Slowed my motion and put all 5 delicious piggies in my mouth. Greedily I filled my mouth; I stopped, and then extended my hot tongue to lick her sweet arches, and watched with pleasure! I was ready for more! There were so many wonderful things to play with seeing her body lay there wanting... waiting was like a kid being the only one at an amusement park! What do I ride first?! I thought. Her huge sweat covered bosom would be my next stop. While she sat near exhaustion on the floor, I placed myself between her voluminous orbs; Rockin' back and forth using all of their softness for my pleasure... my heavy upstroke teased her juicy lips as she licked him until he disappeared into her deep cleavage. Her mouth wanted me... but I remembered her skills so I grabbed her hair and began to slowly drive my spirit into throat depths... deeper and harder. She pulled away and covered her mouth, but she simply couldn't hold back! Now the carpet was wet from her mouths explosion! In the heat of the moment I let her catch her breath and then I guided her back to work. As the intensity heightened I grabbed her magnificent silver hair and pulled it back so that I could look into her big Bambi eyes, and it came right off! Muthafuka! (I thought) My silver haired goddess was a wig wearing imposter! Now I'm looking' at her and she's looking' at me... both speechless about the revelation. The woman I *thought* was my age was gone and there *she* was! Well, after the shock no words were spoken, I led her onto my big ottoman, as she knelt on top of it, I slowly entered... grabbed a handful of her now jet black hair... pulled it back as if it were a mares' reigns and punished her with myself. She had to know that an old man made her tap the fuck out! And she did.

Three's a Crowd

After our mind-blowing session, Stevi; she and I talked a few more times. One night, I was hanging out with Linda. We called Stevi to ask if *she* would like to come out and play. She was game, so 20 minutes later, Linda and I went to pick her up. We stopped for drinks. I knew the notion of our emerging triad was a stretch for Stevi but I felt that, if nothing else, she should have a good night out. We had a great time and returned to my place for the after party. Linda enjoyed watching my conquests, and Stevi was no exception.

After a few more cocktails, Linda and I got started. She wanted me to pay tribute to her with my tongue, and I happily obliged. When I came up for air, there was Stevi, fondling Linda's big, french vanilla toned breasts. I continued to please Linda. Stevi joined in, and gently nudged my head out of the way so that she could indulge in Linda's gifts. The sight of Linda squirming and Stevi's deep, ravenous moans sent my passion into overdrive!

I took Stevi from behind slowly and deliberately, so as not to break her rhythm. With a playful resentment, I wrapped my hand in her hair and pulled her head towards me. Linda kissed and caressed Stevi's dangling bosom while tickling her own fancy. I hit it harder and harder, double-time, as the first beads of sweat rolled down my forehead.

I pulled away from Stevi and prepared myself for Linda. Safety first! Once inside her, I massaged her grace in harmony with every stroke, knowing from experience that she would explode again and again, and again. As Stevi caressed Linda's body, Linda filled her mouth with Stevi's chocolaty goodness. Linda's screams were muffled by Stevi's voluminous breasts. We continued well into the night, culminating in what we all wanted – for them both to be caught in the shower of my explosion. Exhausted, we all tidied up and hit the sack, together. I fell asleep thinking, "THIS is perfect!"

Morning, however, was a different story. Even though we'd had a spectacular night, Stevi had apparently replayed the events in her mind. She was having second thoughts. She was feeling uneasy.

Much to my chagrin, and when I opened my eyes, Stevi was already dressed; she had even called a cab. Dazed and confused, she left without answers; I walked her out as Linda watched. That was the first time Stevi left. And, it was the first Linda watched me run after somebody – ANYBODY! Although I didn't know it at the time these concurrent events would come back to haunt me.

Over time, Stevi's anxiety waned. She and I grew closer. I felt like she really understood me. We talked a lot, and I even granted her a one-on-one with my *little boy*. But, as Stevi and I grew closer, Linda's resentment began to build – perhaps because of the quality of time I spent with Stevi. Until Stevi, no one stayed with me for multiple nights, cooked meals in my kitchen, and received constant attention from me except Linda. And, even though, in *my* mind our relationship was strong, the *woman* in Linda began to cry. Shades of monogamy slowly set in. No longer was I out partying night after night. I spent my free time with Stevi. Eventually, I didn't party at all.

But, Stevi noticed that my light had dimmed. Some of my spark seemed to fade. We decided that reopening the doors and allowing playtime with others would, reignite my flame. I was so far gone though, that I didn't even try to find any playmates. So I was a little surprised when Stevi told me that she had two dates for the weekend! Literally one day after she'd made her *suggestion*. I was cool with it. We'd had a mature discussion about the *rules of engagement,* and we agreed that all systems were go! She claimed that she wasn't even interested in one of the guys – physically – and that she'd met the other on social media. She just "really wanted to go out" and reassured me there was "no need for concern". Surprisingly, I didn't speak with her for whole 3 DAYS! She left on the date and was not answering her phone! When she did finally surface, she said that she had been with the social media guy for the weekend, Stevi apologized profusely for breaking our agreement, and we mended our bond with an awe-inspiring night of makeup sex. Despite that, I began to realize that I was giving to someone who was clear on how to receive.

Linda heard this story and was incensed, but successfully refrained from busting Stevi's head! Despite the fact that she was hurting inside, she genuinely hated the very thought of my being mistreated. Linda stood by me even though, by that time, she figured I was so hooked on Stevi that I'd keep going' back for more.

Stevi and I eased back into a state of normalcy, but she and I still bumped heads. What's worse, the consequences of my actions were weighing on me; I began to resent what I had done. I had taken a life of honesty and trust and reduced it a heaping pile of bullshit. How could I have let this happen? Stevi walked out on me repeatedly – more than 20 times – and for some reason, I always let her back in. Why? I didn't know.

A year and a half later, what was left? My relationship with Linda was strained, to say the least. She was happily dating someone else. Stevi was pregnant with someone else's child; seems that while I was struggling through my mixed emotions she'd met someone at work who made her "feel good."

And Then There Were NONE

So there I stood in the middle of the wreckage – processing – deconstructing and reconstructing the events that led me to that time and space, assimilating all the things I'd learned. And still pondering the questions: Why had I been so vulnerable to bullshit after all I'd been through? Why had I forsaken the unconditional love I'd been searching for for so long? And, *how* can I grow from this?

For now, all I can do is have the presence of mind to heal. I've always believed that it's extremely selfish to involve someone in your emotional storms, so I give myself time.

I've heard women say that the reason they have more than one child is because they forget the pains of childbirth and in love with the lives they've created. It's the forgetfulness that allows their minds and bodies to go back to endure the pain again. The journeys of love and life are no different. I've found that after you've completed each leg of this rat-race, and absorbed its lessons, you forget all the bullshit. For this reason, I forget the sting of treachery, anguish of uncertainty, and the bitter taste of infidelity. The only thing that remains is the *goodness* that drew me to my exes in the first place – qualities that made me stand up and fight for them, the virtues that I truly love – their inner beauty.

I've come to understand that, despite the pain, I have to forgive. I must forgive myself first, and exonerate the ladies who've come and gone in order for me to value, and truly respect the *love*. After all, these women did not join forces and conspire against me, or I against them. I can't fault someone for being who they are. People grow. They evolve and become better human beings. So, selflessly I forgive and hope that I too have been forgiven.

Onward

In the beginning I talked about *championships*, and the notion that, perhaps, I haven't won any - not in the traditional progression from girlfriend, to fiancée, to wife. So, at this point, I have to assess the value of my consolation prizes. These rewards aren't just coupons or gift cards. Rather, they are, precious keepsakes, rooted in what I consider authenticity. Love, good or bad, right or wrong, is my souvenir.

Real love is both simple *and* complex. You love me, I love you. That's it. It's a wonderful gift - put a bow on it! Digging deeper, I've found the nuances that make love so complex. The conditions that surround love are stringent. The solemn vows, spoken before God, are often worth far less than the paper on which certificate of marriage is written.

I, human beings, still love. I can't say that I get better at loving; and I've heard that you can't choose who you love. I have discovered that you can use what you've learned to filter out things that aren't going to work for you, and physically, spiritually and emotionally. Thus, enabling you to make a better choice on who you share your love with. Ultimately, my goal is to love – truly.

But, what *is* true love? Agreements, compromises; an amalgamation of mental, physical, emotional, spiritual connectivity? All of the above; each is necessary, and the nucleus is TRUTH – not the distorted half-truths steeped in persuasion, advancement, and justification – the pure, unadulterated TRUTH. This kind of truth informs, creating choices and building security, despite – and perhaps in light of – the revelation of one's insecurities.

For me, love and truth are like conjoined twins, suffering through a natural relationship of interdependence to achieve an unyielding balance. Love is just and purposeful. And it's out there, waiting for us all - *if* we chose to embrace it – *truthfully*.

Today, I am in tune with all but one of my exes – Jasmine. And yes, I even see some of them occasionally. Linda and I are still best friends, enjoying a closeness that grows and nourishes us both.

One More For The Road

Recently, I went to a poetry slam, and as I pulled up, I saw a stunningly sexy woman walking into the venue. She had beautiful shapely legs and a hypnotic walk. I heard my inner-voice speak to me, saying, "am gonna find her when I get in." While standing at the bar talking to a friend, the woman walked up and said, "Hey stranger!" To my surprise, it was Elle. I sipped my cocktail and ran my fingers slowly across the brim of my black Corleone hat, wondering what this *chance* would bring. *Forever* was waiting, again. Its 7:28p.m *this* is my life.

FOREVER AGAIN

BENJAMIN GREGGORY

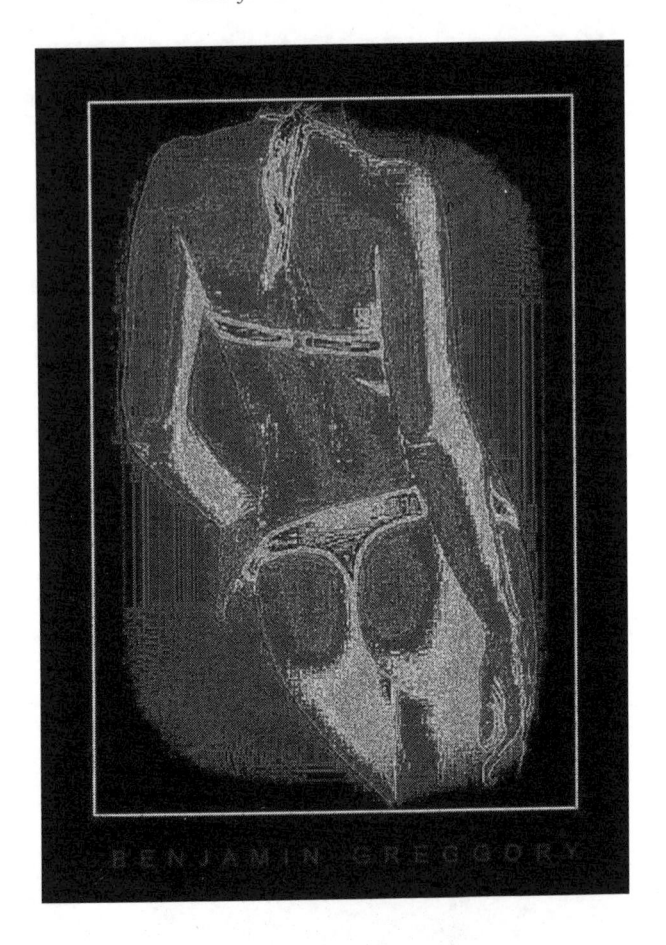

FOREVER AGAIN

BENJAMIN GREGGORY

I would sincerely like to thank the people who have supported my efforts in finishing this book. My Mother, you exposed the world to me and made me look beyond project walls. My sister, you hold me down every day; you are simply the best! My V.A, you continue to redefine both love and friendship. My Aunt, I deeply appreciate your guidance and sacrifice. My Uncle, I continue to grow from your teachings. Jae, what an inspiration you are to me and countless others. Ms. Ina, through your mentorship I have accomplished my goal! To all those who gave me feedback and strength; I humbly *Thank You!*

Made in the USA
Lexington, KY
26 April 2018